O GOD

*The Gospel of Christ's Defeat
of Demons, Sin, and Death*

ANDREW STEPHEN DAMICK

ANCIENT FAITH PUBLISHING
CHESTERTON, INDIANA

Arise, O God: The Gospel of Christ's Defeat of Demons, Sin, and Death
Copyright © 2021 Andrew Stephen Damick

Published by:
  Ancient Faith Publishing
  A Division of Ancient Faith Ministries
  P.O. Box 748
  Chesterton, IN 46304

ISBN: 978-1-955890-02-1

Library of Congress Control Number: 2021942004

Printed in the United States of America

Hannah,

May The LORD illumine your mind, heart, soul, and being always!

Love In Christ, Sahar + Marie Giacobbe

24 . 2022

For Evangelia

and

In memory of
Sandy Damick
(1953–2014)

Contents

God has taken his place in the divine council;
in the midst of the gods he holds judgment:

"How long will you judge unjustly
and show partiality to the wicked?

Give justice to the weak and the fatherless;
maintain the right of the afflicted and the
destitute.

Rescue the weak and the needy;
deliver them from the hand of the wicked."

They have neither knowledge nor
understanding,
they walk about in darkness;
all the foundations of the earth are shaken. `

I say, "You are gods,
sons of the Most High, all of you;
nevertheless, you shall die like men,
and fall like any prince."

Arise, O God, judge the earth;
for to thee belong all the nations!

Psalm 82 (RSV)

Preface

It might be near the height of hubris to write a book about the gospel. I am not, however, writing this because I think I have a special revelation. Rather, it seems to me that there is a need to express the character and content of the gospel in an Orthodox Christian way that can be understood by modern English readers and that is not currently available.

Over the years, as I have struggled to find a way to express the gospel as part of being a pastor, teacher, and communicator, I knew that I would eventually have to compile these thoughts into a coherent whole. I am not claiming that this book is the only way to present the gospel nor the last word on it. It is, however, my best understanding of it and in many ways represents a significant correction or expansion on how I have understood it in the past.

So who exactly is my audience here? I would, of course, like to say "all mankind," but I think this book is best suited to three groups of people: (1) those who are not familiar or only a little familiar with what Christianity is, (2) those who are being catechized (trained to be Christians) within churches, and (3) those who have been catechized and want to go deeper in their Christian faith.

I hope this book will be a tool in the hands of parents, clergy, catechists, and seminarians, and I also hope that it will be able to stand alone fairly well without much contextualization. It is not intended to be a full catechesis but rather to spur the reader toward catechesis. In short, this book addresses why someone would even *want* to be catechized.

A note for non-Christians: In this book, you will see many references to passages from the Bible (e.g., "John 3:16"). I understand that you may not see the Bible as authoritative in the way Christians do, but these references are there to help the reader further explore particular content.

A note for all: I write (as best as I am able) from the point of view of the Orthodox Church, but I do not regard the content of this book as being the Orthodox "version" of the gospel of Jesus Christ. It is simply the gospel. The gospel doesn't have versions.

All errors here are my own, and I welcome correction and ask for your prayers.

Fr. Andrew Stephen Damick
Emmaus, Pennsylvania
Annunciation 2021

What Is Not the Gospel?

*"Excuse me, but do you have a minute
to talk about our Lord and Savior
Jesus Christ?"*

Even if you have no experience with Christianity, you have probably heard the word *gospel*, and you may well have heard that it has something to do with "being saved." So the gospel is something you listen to and buy into if you want to get saved. Here in twenty-first–century America (my context), the gospel as usually preached and generally understood is essentially a kind of sales pitch, and the product you are encouraged to buy is eternal life.

For most people now, this is what the preaching

of the gospel looks like. It is not surprising, therefore, that a lot of people tune out the sales pitch. In the developed world, we are the targets of hundreds of advertisements every day, and everything advertised—from toothpaste to telephone service to taco delivery—promises, if not quite eternal life, at least to change your life.

Everything now is the Best Thing Ever, at least since the last Best Thing. If we believed every ad we see and hear, we could have a conversion experience several times a day. It is no wonder that the sales-pitch gospel is easy to ignore and that the religion attached to it is often the butt of jokes.

I want to begin by addressing what the gospel is *not*, because I want to make it clear that this book is *not* about what usually goes by "the gospel" in our time and place. This book is *not* about the sales pitch. But I think we need to understand what the sales-pitch gospel communicates and where it comes from so that we can at least not mistake it for the real thing.

The Bible, which is a witness to the gospel, refers to it as "the power of God" (Rom. 1:16), a "mystery" (Eph. 6:19), and "the word of the truth" (Col. 1:5). It is hardly something so trivial as a product to be pitched, bought, and sold.

Economic activity is not always trivial, of course, but the act of *marketing*—communicating in a way designed to elicit buy-in—does something to our perception of what is being marketed. It suggests that the product is within our control.

If something is marketed to me, it is implicitly being communicated that this thing is subject to my choice, to my desires. Whether I leave it aside or take it up, it is because I am the greater thing. I am the consumer. I am the customer. And the customer is always right.

When religion is marketed, we get the sense of being manipulated, of being deceived. I have even seen fake currency (in large denominations, of course), left as or with a tip for wait staff at a restaurant, that turns out to be a religious tract when turned over. Whoever designed that tract actually imagined it was a good idea to make someone think he was picking up money but to give him a deceptive, manipulative product pitch instead.

And when the product is eternal life, that sense of manipulation is understandably increased: I am supposed to give up my time, effort, and money, not to mention possibly my friends, family, or social position—and in some circumstances, my freedom or even my life—in exchange for something I won't get until after I'm dead? That fine print of *No Refunds or Exchanges* sounds especially ominous.

Is it any wonder that the preaching of the gospel in the twenty-first-century world so often falls flat, comes across as tiresome, controlling, and fake? Is it any wonder that calling the gospel "good news" can draw mockery in response?

At least the salesman pitching me a vacuum cleaner has something solid and material in his hands that will solve one of my problems when I turn it on. And if he's selling a bad product, I can always report him to the Better Business Bureau. But to whom do you report a defective spiritual product?

How Did the Gospel Become a Sales Pitch?

So how did we get here? Why is the gospel now understood as basically an economic exchange, so that the appropriate way to encourage people to make that exchange is to market it?

I will not go deep into the historical and doctrinal details here (if you're interested in that, see my book *Orthodoxy and Heterodoxy*), but the short version is this: In the sixteenth century, the major religious question being asked by the new Christian movement called the Protestant Reformation was, "What must I do to be saved?" It's a good question, and it's a question asked in the Bible itself (Acts 16:30). But that question and its answer are not what the gospel is, not according to the Bible and certainly not in the way the Bible was understood for most of Christian history.

If you read the biblical narrative closely, you will see that laudable question is a *response* to the gospel being preached. It is not itself the gospel. And the answer to that question is not the gospel, either. So what happens to the gospel when you make that question and its answer the *content* of the gospel rather than the *response* to it?

When you define the gospel as "how you get saved," the gospel shifts into the realm of the *individual quest for salvation*. And if becoming and being a Christian (what you do when you believe the gospel) is an individual quest, then persuading me of why I need to be on that quest (what is sin and how can it be fixed?) and explaining what rightly pursuing the quest looks like will finally require a kind of sales pitch.

Why? It is because the gospel has come to be about my individual problem and the individual solution to my problem. So if I agree I have a problem and then agree to the solution, I need to commit to what it takes to get that solution.

Almost every advertisement naturally follows that pattern: Tell the customer he has a problem (which he might not have known he had), tell him the solution to his problem, and then encourage him to buy the solution from you.

Compounding this individualization of the gospel is the transactional character of the way the problem was conceived at the time of the Reformation (for both Protestants and Catholics): God's divine justice has to be satisfied, so humans have to bring something—good works, pure belief, sacramental participation, etc., depending on a particular group's theology—to the table in order to come away with salvation in exchange.

Later revivalist movements in American Protestantism made use of emotional techniques to pressure the potential convert to make an individual *decision* for Christ. This decision came to be regarded as the key moment when someone became a Christian and (in many theologies) was seen as what got them on their way to eternal life in heaven.

Such emotional techniques were not seen as dishonest at all but were instead considered proper gospel preaching that helped people see what their problem was and that Jesus was the only solution. And these techniques eventually came to be used for advertising all kinds of products that had no particular connection with Christianity.

I could say much more here about the details of how these theologies work out in particular communities, but suffice it for our purposes here to say that this history is how we got to where we are now. As generally understood in the culture, the gospel is a kind of product, and Christians are basically Jesus' (or, if you are really cynical, religious leaders') customers. These customers give their time, talent, and treasure—and in more extreme cases, their freedom or their lives—and in return, they get to go to heaven after they die.

I believe this conception of the gospel is simply wrong, and most of the rest of this book will be devoted to describing what the gospel really is. The last section will discuss the response to the gospel. I hope it will be clear by that point that the response is not what the gospel is, and it's not even about each of us as individuals.

"How do I get saved?" is not the gospel. And "So, would you like to get saved?" is not preaching the gospel.

This book is not a sales pitch. I hope that instead it will be an authentic, true proclamation of the gospel. How or whether you respond to it is important, but I'm not going to make a marketing appeal to you at the end.

Knowing what the gospel is and being able to teach it to someone else does not require that you know everything in this book. But by the end of it, you should know what a gospel is, why there is a gospel at all, what the gospel is, and what the response to it requires.

CHAPTER 1

What Is a Gospel?

*But I know that when I come to you, I shall
come in the fullness of the blessing of the
gospel of Christ. (Romans 15:29)*

Near the dawn of the first century, a stone-mason tapped his hammer and chisel on a
rock in Priene, a city on the southwestern shore
of the Roman province of Asia (now in southwest
Turkey). Cooled by the sea breezes of the eastern
Aegean, he was tapping out a long gospel text in
ancient Greek, carving it into stone for all who
were literate to stop, read, believe, and obey.[1]

---

1 For details on the Roman sense of *evangelia*, including
the inscription from Priene, see Wright, N. T., *Paul and
the Faithfulness of God* (Minneapolis: Fortress Press,

This was not the first time the Greek-speaking city of Priene had heard this gospel, however. Before our ancient mason began his work, a Roman herald had ridden into the city, opened up a scroll, and started preaching the gospel.

This gospel spoke of the birth of a savior, whom providence had arranged to be filled with virtue for the benefit of all mankind. This savior, given to those who heard the gospel and their descendants, was bringing an end to all war. If it had not been for him, the whole world would have met its ruin.

His benefactions were greater than those of all previous benefactors, and no one would ever surpass what he had done. The birth of this divine one was therefore the beginning of the good news (*evangelia*) for the whole world. His birthday would be celebrated as a fundamental change to the whole order of the cosmos. This proclamation was not, however, the gospel of Jesus Christ. The year was 9 BC, and this was the gospel of Augustus Caesar, the first emperor of the Roman Empire.

2013), pp. 325–328.

Gospel Is a Pre-Christian Genre

Before we get to the content of *the* gospel, that is, the gospel of Jesus Christ and His Kingdom, we should discuss what the word itself means. That is, what is *a* gospel?

In our time, *gospel* is a religious word. It is also used metaphorically, referring to something that ought to be believed as "the gospel truth," whatever its content. Or we may refer to something that people believe in passionately as their "gospel," for example, "the gospel of libertarian economics." But these are understood as metaphors, and *gospel* in its literal usage is now a religious term, specifically Christian.

That was how I understood *gospel* when I was growing up. It was not until well into adulthood that I learned that *evangelion*—the Greek word used in the New Testament that gets translated into English as "gospel"—actually had a pre-Christian and even (in a sense) a non-religious origin. (In the ancient world, however, religion couldn't really be separated from everything else.) Literally, *evangelion* means "good news," but in its actual ancient usage it meant more than that. The etymology does not exhaust the way the word was understood when the apostles used it in the New Testament. We may be tempted to look at the etymology of a word or the meaning of its constituent parts and think we've got its meaning locked down.

But consider a word like *breakfast*, which at one time was literally about breaking a fast— that is, the fast one had been keeping since one went to sleep. But no one now uses the word that way. *Breakfast* is simply the morning meal, the first meal of the day, and almost no one wakes up and thinks to himself, "I've been fasting. Time to break that fast."

Or consider the English word *butterfly*. Etymologically, the *butter* part might come from the color of certain species of butterfly. Or it might derive from a folk belief that this insect stole butter. But *butterfly* isn't about butter, and it's not about flies. We all know what a butterfly is, and it's not because we combined *butter* and *fly*. (Of course, we could make this even more complicated by mentioning the phrase *butterflies in my stomach*.)

The reason we know what *breakfast* and *butterfly* mean is that those terms are in common use. Most English speakers use them all the time, and we know what they mean because of the way we use them. The situation with *evangelion* in the time of Jesus is the same. Even though *evangelion* in its two parts literally translates as "good news," we can't assume that phrase exhausts what the term means. Certainly, the gospel of Jesus Christ is good news! And it is a good thing for Christians to reflect on what it means that the gospel is good news. But that is not its whole meaning, or even most of it. And if we think that *evangelion* is only good news (even the best news ever), then we risk falling into that sales pitch: *Have I got good news for you!*

It turns out that *evangelion* had a popular, technical meaning in the first-century Greco-Roman context, a specific meaning that everyone in that time and place understood. They had heard many evangelia in their time. An evangelion was a kind of "good news," but it was a specific genre with a specific kind of content.

When the writers of the Christian Gospels—Ss. Matthew, Mark, Luke, and John—referred to their works as *gospels*, they weren't simply saying they were writing books about some good news. They chose the word *evangelion* and intended by it what the world around them had already been using it for. So what did the rest of the world mean by it?

The first thing we should know about the word *evangelion* as used in the first-century Greco-Roman culture into which the gospel was first preached is that it almost always appeared in the plural—*evangelia*, or as we might say, "gospels." This plural did not refer to a set of books, though, as when Christians say "the four Gospels." Rather, evangelia were announcements people heard in public, proclaimed loudly in the streets by a professional herald and sometimes inscribed in stone so that they might be preserved.

And what was that herald talking about? He was most often talking about military victories. *Gospel* wasn't what we would call a religious word. It was a military one.

Evangelia were proclamations of titles and accomplishments declared by heralds when their masters—usually generals or governors, but sometimes Roman senators or Caesar himself— were about to ride into the city. They were not advertisements or sales pitches. They were basically warnings.

Someone important (and often dangerous)

was on his way, and the evangelia were lists covering both who he was and what he had accomplished in war. So you had better be ready.

And if it was Caesar (or his representative) coming to town, the list of evangelia was often comically long and enormously inflated (at least from our point of view). But it did have a religious character. Besides listing his military victories, the evangelia would proclaim Caesar to be a god, "the son of a god," and even "the savior of the world." The Priene inscription mentioned above includes exactly this language.

The idea that a political leader should make such claims for himself sounds ridiculous to us now (though that doesn't stop some people from treating politicians as if they were saviors and gods). But we should recall two things: (1) great people in the first century were understood as having a god or spirit connected to them (even the philosopher Socrates referred to his personal *daemon*), and (2) the Roman Caesar ruled over most of what was understood to be "the world." So when, in the Priene inscription, Augustus was declared the divine savior of the world, people took that claim seriously.

It was Caesar's divine greatness that had

enabled him to bring the *Pax Romana* (Roman peace) to so much of the world, saving it from civil war, barbarity, and chaos. And at that time, no one had even invented the idea of the separation of church (or religion) and state. Religion was a key component of political life. Or, to put it another way, politics was a key component of religious life.

People *expected* Caesar to be divine, if not actually a god. Who could have accomplished something so great without divinity being involved? No one had ever seen so much of the world united under one ruler. And in the ancient world being a ruler, even of a small territory, was understood to imply close association with a divine spirit.

A gospel in that time and place therefore was a proclamation of the one being proclaimed and what he had done. But there was always a third element to these evangelia—what was expected of those receiving the message.

In the case of the Priene inscription, which is often referred to as the *Calendar Inscription of Priene*, a new civil year was being proclaimed. The birthday of Augustus on September 23 would be celebrated as a holiday and would also be the day when all civil magistrates would take office. Life in the cities of Asia under the empire would be reordered according to this proclamation. And although this is not stated in the preserved inscriptions, it was certainly understood that Caesar expected those living within his empire to be obedient to him, not to rebel, and to count him as their only king.

It seems that in Asia at the time, a competition was held to see what the best way of honoring the birth of Augustus would be. The Roman proconsul, the highest official in the province, won it with his suggestion of the calendar change. To us today, this might seem like a strange way to win the competition, but consider what this means: The birth of Augustus is of cosmic importance, so significant that the rhythms of life itself are altered for both the individual and the whole community.

Calendars affect everything and everyone both singularly and collectively, and so Caesar's presence is now immediately and always felt. For someone proclaimed to be divine, what clearer statement could there be about the momentousness of his coming? In a sense, the sun and moon and stars themselves (also understood to be divine) now move with the rhythm of Caesar.

This gospel had such profound implications that it was engraved on white marble and prominently displayed in the precincts of the temple in Priene, a temple dedicated to Roma (a goddess personifying the city of Rome and its empire) and to Augustus. The people of Asia were expected to offer worship in response, and this worship was not merely adulation for the emperor but a way of binding them to him. Although Augustus was often careful to have himself referred to by the Latin *divus* ("divine" or "deified") rather than *deus* ("god"), the lack of a true Greek equivalent for the former would have made the collapse of the two into the Greek *theos* ("god") natural.[2] Thus, in the gospel inscription at Priene, Augustus is referred to not only as *theos* but as *theotatos* ("extremely divine"), suggesting that the

---

2   Wright, 327. He writes here in a footnote that *divus* had a wide range of meaning over time, so even though the Greek *theios* ("divine," "godlike") was used for emperors, the original meaning of *divus* seems to have even been "higher" than *deus*, referring to those who had always been divine rather than divinized humans. Much later, *divus* applied to emperors meant simply "dead." He concludes that for Augustus, at any rate, *theios* was not equivalent to *divus*.

distinction wasn't being taken too seriously. After all, who but a god could have accomplished all this?

The ultimate in "gospel" in the ancient Roman world was the proclamation of a divine emperor whose coming meant that time itself was going to be reordered, who had conquered his enemies and established peace throughout the world's largest empire, and who now expected worship and obedience in response.

Now, imagine if that Roman herald, instead of proclaiming his Augustan gospel in the streets of Priene—a gospel that would eventually be inscribed on white marble in the temple—approached someone on the street and asked, "Do you have a moment to talk about what Augustus Caesar can do for your life?"

It sounds ridiculous. No one would have called that real *evangelia*. No one would have taken it seriously. The kinds of claims Augustus was making about himself, who he was and what he had accomplished, and the expectations of worship and obedience that he laid upon his empire, would never be taken seriously as a sales pitch.

These were not products to be offered for sale. They were fundamentally a claim about a change in the world and what you had to do if you were going to be part of it. Going against that constituted rebellion. And the Roman response to disobedience was to expel rebels from their world, usually by execution, conquest, or massacre.

Not Caesar's Gospel but Christ's

With all that in mind, consider the opening words of Mark's Gospel:

> *The beginning of the gospel of Jesus Christ, the Son of God. (Mark 1:1)*

If you swap out *Jesus Christ* there for *Augustus Caesar*, you have almost exactly the same claim being made, in almost the same language. I have no idea whether St. Mark had ever heard of the inscription in Priene, but he certainly knew that throughout the Roman Empire Augustus was acclaimed the son of a god and the savior of the world, and his birth was heralded as the beginning of *evangelia*. So when St. Mark, living in the small Roman province of Judea, wrote this line in his own Gospel, it was an act of rebellion against Rome.

And the other Gospel writers did essentially the same thing. When they referred to their texts as *gospels*, they were invoking this existing Roman concept of the *evangelia*. But each of them, and indeed other writers throughout the New Testament as well, said they were writing not *evangelia* in the plural but rather the *evangelion* in the singular.

In other words, this was *the* gospel, the one and only. All other gospels were false. All other gospels were being defeated and thrown down. The gospel of Caesar was ending, and the proclamation was beginning of the coming of the King of kings Himself, who ruled not only an empire but the whole cosmos.

It is Jesus who is the Son of God, not Caesar. It is Jesus who is divine, not Caesar. It is Jesus who is the Savior of the world, not Caesar. It is Jesus whose birth changed time forever, not Caesar. Jesus is the One whose benefactions to mankind are the greatest and will never be surpassed, the One whose coming is for all who receive Him and their descendants, the One who will bring peace and because of whom the world will not fall into ruin—Jesus, not Caesar.

We will further explore this later, but we

should note that the gospel of Jesus Christ is not at its core a response to the gospel of Augustus Caesar. In the New Testament the *genre* of gospel is being used to declare the coming of Jesus Christ. But the declaration itself is not aimed at conquering Caesar and his empire, except by implication. There will of course be no room for any other kingdoms in the wake of the coming of Jesus' Kingdom.

The declaration, which is good news for mankind, is explicitly an act of aggression against the domination of a different kingdom that had spread throughout the whole world—one more expansive than the Roman Empire, a kingdom not ruled by human beings. The gospel of Jesus Christ is, in essence, an assault on the kingdom of the demons.

As St. Paul puts it, "For we do not wrestle against flesh and blood, but against principalities, against powers, against the rulers of the darkness of this age, against spiritual *hosts* of wickedness in the heavenly *places*" (Eph. 6:12 NKJV). The purpose of Jesus' coming into the world was not to declare war against any human kingdom but rather against a demonic one. The defeated enemies whose overthrow is primary among the accomplishments in the gospel of Jesus Christ are demonic enemies.

The gospel of Jesus Christ is the announcement of the inauguration of a kingdom, the very thing Christians pray for in the Lord's Prayer when they say "Thy kingdom come." Indeed, in the Lord's Prayer, we can see all three of the declarative elements that are included in the gospel genre: (1) who the one being proclaimed is, (2) what he has accomplished, and (3) what he expects of his subjects. So let's use this most well-known of Christian prayers to summarize everything we have said in this chapter:

> *Our Father, who art in heaven, hallowed be Thy name. Thy kingdom come, Thy will be done on earth as it is in heaven. Give us this day our daily bread, and forgive us our trespasses as we forgive those who trespass against us. And lead us not into temptation, but deliver us from the evil one. (Matt. 6:9–13, Luke 11:2–4)*

Who is being proclaimed? "Our Father, who art in heaven"—this is God Himself who is being proclaimed. "Hallowed be Thy name"—He is the holy One, the One whose name is above all other names.

What has He accomplished? "Thy will be done on earth as it is in heaven"—He has subjected the whole creation to Himself.[3] "Give us this day our daily bread"—He provides all their sustenance. "Forgive us our trespasses"—He has released His people from the slavery of sin. "Lead us not into temptation"—He shows His people the right way of living. "But deliver us from the evil one"—He has rescued His people from the domination of the devil.

What does He expect? "Thy kingdom come"— His rule will be the sole rule among us. "Thy will be done on earth as it is in heaven"—He expects

---

3   While worded in English as a prayer about humanity on earth aligning with the obedience of heaven, this prayer reveals a "both now and not yet" scenario so common in Scripture, as seen in Matt. 28:18–19: "And Jesus came and spoke to them, saying, 'All authority has been given to Me in heaven and on earth. Go therefore and make disciples of all the nations, baptizing them in the name of the Father and of the Son and of the Holy Spirit.'" Because this authority has been returned to Him, His disciples are now sent out to make that authority effective throughout the world. The prayer is synergistic, with human obedience predicated on divine accomplishment.

obedience, and it should be performed here on earth just as it is in heaven, human beings mirroring the angels. "Forgive us our trespasses as we forgive those who trespass against us"—obedience requires forgiving others, which is imitating Him, and being forgiven depends on being forgiving.

This is the prayer that Jesus Himself gave to His followers and that has been used as a model for prayer ever since. Note what is absent: the sense that the Christian life is about answering the question "What must I do to be saved?" That question is of course implied as a response to the content of this prayer, but it is not included in it. Rather, the prayer is itself a declaration of the gospel.

We will finish this book by asking "What must I do to be saved?" But first we have to understand what that question is a response to. And we also have to understand what it is we're being saved from, what problem the gospel proclamation was intended to address. Let's now turn to that latter question, which is: Why is there a gospel?

CHAPTER 2

Why Is There a Gospel?

*This is a faithful saying and worthy of all
acceptance, that Christ Jesus came into the
world to save sinners, of whom I am chief.
(1 Timothy 1:15)*

When gospels were declared in the streets
of ancient cities, it is because those cities had been dominated by some other power,
and now a new power was coming to assert rule.
If the previous rulers had been oppressive, this
gospel was indeed good news. And of course any
conqueror having his gospel proclaimed would
describe the previous rulers as oppressors and
himself as a liberator. No one had his herald
announce that he was coming to dominate and

enslave the city. That would not have been good news at all.

In the gospel of Augustus Caesar, his herald announced that war was coming to an end. The ancient world saw a lot of war, and if an empire ought to offer anything, it would be peace. What would be the point of combining numerous kingdoms under a single ruler if strife continued?

Likewise, Augustus promised that his coming would bring other benefits to the people under his rule. Not only was he saving the world from war and from domination by other rulers, he was also bringing blessings. Life would be better under Augustus. And while life in the Roman Empire was not exactly comfortable by modern standards, especially for the majority who were non-citizens, the Romans generally did bring peace, along with roads, better trade, public order, medicine, and sanitation.

This is not to say that life was really that great for the average person in the empire. If you were a non-citizen (in Latin, *non persona*; you weren't seen as a person), you had no real rights. For instance, a soldier from the local garrison could kill non-citizens or take a woman or child for unspeakable purposes with impunity. The

Romans were often brutal to the non-Romans living in their empire.

Yet while plebeians (particularly women and children) didn't have it good anywhere in the world at the time, if you had to be a plebeian somewhere, the Roman Empire was probably the best place to be. Being part of the empire did not make you *a* Roman (citizenship was reserved for relatively few people), but it probably made you *more* Roman.

Roman culture, technology, wealth, and order touched everyone in the empire, even the slaves, who were lower in status than the plebeians. If you lived within Roman boundaries, you experienced and at least in some ways benefited from Roman rule.

So when the gospel of Augustus was preached, it wasn't empty promises. Being part of his empire meant receiving something real. But most of all, it meant that you belonged to him now. Your previous rulers were either subjugated or destroyed. In the empire, every knee had to bow to Caesar and confess him as lord.

This sense that the gospel was announcing a good change in the world is part of the genre imported into the gospel of Jesus Christ.

Augustus's gospel meant, above all, that the *Pax Romana* was being spread throughout the world. There would be peace. So what change did the gospel of Jesus herald?

The gospel of Jesus Christ came to mankind because of three kinds of domination by hostile powers, which resulted from three events described in Genesis. Genesis is the first book of the Bible, the collection of books that witnesses to the events that lead up to, include, and flow from the proclamation of the gospel. These three events collectively make up what in Christian theology is commonly called "the Fall."

In most presentations of the gospel in our time, only one of these three event/effect pairs is typically mentioned as the Fall, because of the reduction of the gospel to the question of how one is saved. But a proper understanding of the gospel has to include all three. So let's now look at what these three events are and the effects they had so that we can understand why there is a gospel.

The Fall: Death

The first of the three events the gospel addresses is Adam's eating of the forbidden fruit, and the effect it had on him and his descendants was death. Before we get to that event, however, we have to understand something about where Adam came from and why his eating of that fruit mattered.

As recorded in Genesis, God created everything that exists. But before the earth as we now know it was filled with life, there was formless chaos, a void. When God creates, therefore, He brings order to His creation precisely in a *creative* way. I think it's important that we highlight God's *creativity* here, if only because His act of creation is not often described as an act of creativity, an act of artistry. Yet God is presented in Genesis as an artist, an artificer, a maker and shaper of beauty.

And so when God creates the earth, He is designing order, an order that reflects who He is, an order whose internal ways of functioning express His character. It is an act of *going forth* for God to create the world. He made something that is *not Himself* (it is created, and He is uncreated) and *not made out of Himself* (He did not take part of Himself as the building blocks of the world), but which nonetheless *reflects Himself*. This is an act of creativity, the act of an artist.

Even the acts of creation we humans engage in follow this same order, though of course we cannot, like God, create something from nothing. God's creation is initially a creation of chaotic matter out of nothing, but then He makes order from chaotic matter. We likewise make order from chaotic matter in imitation of Him. As professor and fantasy novelist J.R.R. Tolkien once wrote, "We make in our measure and in our derivative mode, because we are made: and not only made, but made in the image and likeness of a Maker."[4]

And this is an important point, because if mankind is the highest and best of God's creation, then mankind ought to reflect God's character more than any other creature. This point is highlighted in Genesis by God saying that He made mankind in His image and likeness, to rule over the creatures of the earth, both plants and animals, and indeed the whole earth itself. Man's purpose, given by God, is to assist Him in His creative project of making order and beauty from chaos, to "image" God

---

4   Tolkien, J.R.R. *Tolkien on Fairy-stories*, Verlyn Flieger and Douglas A. Anderson, eds. (HarperCollins Publishers, 2008), p. 66.

by participating in God's works (Gen. 1:26–30).

Adam participates in God's creativity even before the making of Eve by giving names to all the animals (Gen. 2:19–20), a collaborative act between God and man. This is the beginning of Adam's obedience to God's command to subdue the earth, a royal act on his part. Adam is expressing God's order by bringing order to the animal world.

God brings the animals to Adam "to see what he would call them. And whatever Adam called each living creature, that *was* its name" (Gen. 2:19 NKJV). This synergistic cooperation shows how the relationship between God and man had been designed by God. And this should remind us of how parents foster creativity in their own children, bringing to them the elements they need to exercise their creativity and working with them so they can develop in freedom, to see what they do with what they are given.

So when God makes Adam, He forms him not directly out of nothing but rather out of soil (or dust), bringing order and form to chaos, breathing into him the breath of life and making him a living being (Gen. 2:7).

Then He makes Eve by taking a portion of

Adam's side, so that she will be a proper companion who corresponds to Adam (Gen. 2:21–23). Adam had been commanded to subdue the earth and also fill it (Gen. 1:28), but he could not obey the latter half of the command without Eve. And it is for this reason that marriage is the joining together of a man and a woman (Gen. 2:24)—so that they can create more humans together. God's creation thus reflects who He is and has its proper, ordered functioning built in.

The setting for all this creativity is a garden (or orchard, as some translations have it) planted by God in a place called Eden. God made trees there with many fruits for Adam and Eve to eat, but in the center of the garden stood two trees—the Tree of Life and the Tree of the Knowledge of Good and Evil.

That the setting is a garden is not an arbitrary choice. In the ancient world in which Genesis was first read, people mostly interacted with their gods in two possible settings—gardens or temples, which were often built as towers or ziggurats. (A ziggurat is a terraced, often pyramid-shaped building, usually included in a larger temple structure or compound, on top of which sacrifices were offered to gods.) Gods were understood to live on mountains or in gardens, and so manmade sacred spaces dedicated to their worship were made to resemble these places.

Often temples were placed in the center of a garden, combining the two. And in many cases, these were built at the top of or near a mountain or large hill, often in the center of a city. The famous Hanging Gardens of Babylon consisted of a ziggurat that doubled as a garden—thus, a mountain-shaped temple covered with gardens.

In the center of these ancient gardens was placed an idol, an image of the god whose dedication ceremony included an "opening of the nostrils," where the breath of the god passed into the idol, thus in a sense trapping the god inside it. The idol was then served by its worshipers as a means of controlling the god and getting favors from it. Sacrifices were made to it, offerings of food that were then eaten, constituting a meal shared with the god.

But when God creates man, it is *He* who makes the garden, *He* who sets up an image of Himself, *He* who breathes life into the image, and *He* feeds man rather than being fed by him. This is the opposite of idolatry, in which man attempts to control a god by feeding it. Rather, God makes man and gives him communion and relationship with Himself as an act of divine freedom.

And it is this relationship of communion and collaborative creativity that is marred by the introduction of death to mankind. Before creating Eve, God gives Adam the garden to cultivate and care for (again, acts of cooperation with God), but He also warns Adam not to eat of the Tree of the Knowledge of Good and Evil, because when he eats from it he will die (Gen. 2:15–17).

A question that naturally comes to mind is this one: Is the fruit of that tree poisonous? Why does Adam die when he eats it?

To understand why death comes with that fruit, we have to know something else about the creation at that point: Adam and Eve are not the only intelligent creatures in the world. God has also created what we normally call angels. And "off-camera," so to speak, a rebellion has occurred. We will get to this more later, but for now, this explains why there is a "serpent" speaking to Eve in Genesis 3. That serpent is a manifestation of a rebellious angel, also called a *demon*.

The demon persuaded Eve to eat of the fruit, and she in turn persuaded Adam to do the same. When they did that, they joined in that demonic rebellion against God. And in response, God gave them death. The fruit was not poisonous. Death was given by God.

Death was God's response to this act of rebellion, but it was not given out of revenge. After all, God has no need of anything, so He does not have hurt feelings or a need to get back at Adam for joining the demonic rebellion. Rather, death was given to mankind as a way of defeating God's enemies.

To understand what this means, we have to know something about angels. Angels who rebel against God can never repent. They will never be transformed back into harmony with God. Saint John of Damascus, in his *Exact Exposition of the Orthodox Faith*, says that they cannot repent because they do not have mortal, corruptible bodies. Their nature does not permit them to repent. Repentance is possible only when someone has a mortal, corruptible body.[5]

Saint John does not explain why exactly that is. And we might also ask why angels can't just change their minds, if they have free will. The

---

5 *An Exact Exposition of the Orthodox Faith*, Book II, chapter 3, "Concerning angels."

latter question is perhaps easier to answer: Free will is not the same as freedom of action. You have the ability to harm yourself, but you do not necessarily have the ability to heal yourself. The rebellious angels harmed themselves, but they cannot heal their rebellion.

Like the angels, humanity was created immortal and incorruptible, though not inherently immortal and self-sustaining (only God is so). Humanity is sustained by grace. So if God had left humans as they had been created after they sinned, then their disobedience would have fixed them in permanent rebellion, just as it had fixed the rebellious angels. God cut humans off from the Tree of Life, exiling them from Eden, so that they would not be confirmed and crystallized in rebellion the way the demons had been (Gen. 3:22–24).

So when God gives death to humans, it is so that they can repent, so that they can be transformed to be back in harmony with God. With mortality comes the changeability needed to return to God. In this way, God is permitting those who had defected to the side of the demons to return to Him, to realign with Him and pledge their allegiance again to Him, stealing the victory from the demons. Giving the possibility of repentance to mankind is thus part of how God defeats His enemies the demons, who had rebelled against Him by trying to destroy mankind out of envy for man's destiny in Christ (we will look at this destiny in chapters 5 and 6). This opportunity is given only to mankind, not to the demons (Heb. 2:16).

We will discuss repentance again later, but this should suffice to explain why death was God's response to man's disobedience. And it also introduces the very intimate involvement of demons in all of this.

Man's act of disobedience to God and the death that followed it is what most descriptions of "the Fall" are about, though they usually describe death as a punishment for disobedience. This version of the story implies that the solution is about removing the punishment. But as we will see, there is much more going on. And we should say more here about death.

The problem of the forbidden fruit is not that it was poisonous as such but rather that mankind was not ready for it. The theme of demons (false gods) giving knowledge to mankind for which it is not ready in order to bring about its destruction exists both in the Bible and in other ancient narratives, and this account from Genesis is exactly that type of story. Students of Greek mythology may recall the stories of Prometheus giving fire to mankind and the "gift" of Pandora's Box, both instances of knowledge man is not ready for bringing many evils into the world.

Death comes into God's response to the demon, as well. In Genesis 3:14, God tells the serpent (i.e., the demon) that he will be cast down and eat dust. This element is often explained as the story of why snakes have no legs, but we should remember that this is a demon, not a snake. Snakes don't talk, for one thing. And it's not as if ancient people thought snakes ate dirt. They knew better than that.

What is happening here is that the demon is having all his power stripped from him and is being cast into the underworld, which is traditionally depicted as a place of dust and ash. He has only one power left to him, the power of death. This demon who holds the power of death is identified as the devil (Heb. 2:14). This same passage in Hebrews also mentions that God gives aid to mankind but not to angels (2:16). So we see again here that man's mortality and its eventual cure (more on that later!) are related to the war some angels have declared on God.

Adam and Eve don't know what death is, though, so God kills an animal in front of them to show them what will happen.[6] He clothes them in "garments of skin," which does not mean that they start wearing leather made from the animal just killed, but rather that their bodies become mortal, changing to become like the bodies of animals (which are already mortal).[7] This is the moment when death becomes part of human experience, and it has many implications, including that the simple act of obtaining food will now require hard labor and that childbirth will be painful.

Adam and Eve are expelled from Paradise, which is the presence of God in Eden. Death finds its full expression in Genesis 4, which details the first murder. One of their sons, Cain, kills his brother, Abel. And the Bible doubles and

---

6   This inference from Genesis 3 is made in both the Second Temple Judaism period and in some patristic commentators, such as Ephrem the Syrian's *Commentary on Genesis* 2.33.1. It is not explicit in the text of Genesis, however.

7   Various church fathers hold this view, e.g., Gregory of Nyssa in *On the Soul and the Resurrection*.

trebles (and quadruples, etc.) down on this pattern in Genesis 5, a genealogical record in which every family line finishes with "and he died."

Death now dominates mankind. God gives a kind of mitigation through human fertility,[8] but that only manages the death problem of mankind. It does not cure it.

The Fall: Sin

The second of the events that constitute the Fall is the introduction of sin into mankind. Sin is, simply, "missing the mark," but it is not the same as making a mistake. It is rebellion against God and the law that He wrote into the creation. Because sin is rebellion, because it is harmful, sinners have victims. Being a sinner means I'm harming others and also myself. Sin does not mean merely breaking rules but actually causing

---

8 God knew that death would come to mankind, so from our point of view, fertility was given before the Fall with the Fall nevertheless in mind. Discussion exists within the Orthodox Church about whether fertility would have worked differently before the garments of skin were given, but we will not go into that here. All we know is that reproduction does not happen until after death comes to humanity and that it is a way for mankind to perpetuate itself in the face of death.

harm, including harm we may not perceive.

Sin enters into mankind through death, and the fear of death is the occasion of all our sin and our slavery to that fear (Heb. 2:15). What does that mean?

The fear of death may be quite literal. We might harm someone else so that we can escape being killed. But it may also result in our fending off death in more general terms. I might cheat someone because I fear what will happen to me if I don't have everything I want. I might be violent toward someone else out of fear of not getting what I want. I might be cruel toward someone out of fear of having my feelings or privacy impinged on. I might ignore someone out of fear of experiencing someone else's suffering. I might drown my sorrows in drink or indulge in gluttony to stave off feelings of lack. All these are forms of sin based on the fear of death.

Corruptibility also enters mankind through death. While we usually think of *corruption* in moral terms (such as corrupt politicians), it refers more immediately to what happens to mortal human bodies in this world. We can be injured. We can grow sick. We die. And after death, our bodies decay. (That is why some saints' bodies that do not decay after death are referred to as *incorrupt*.)

In the chapters in Genesis that follow the expulsion from Eden, looking especially at the family line of Cain, we see increasing sin. Cain's descendant Lamech is a murderer like his fore-father. Corruption multiplies throughout the world. Demonic beings interact more with man-kind, producing the nephilim and granting more destructive knowledge.[9]

The spread of sinful corruption and interac-tion with demons should underline for us that sin is not a mere matter of violating a rule. It is what we might call an *existential* problem, affect-ing the daily existence of human beings, propel-ling them away from God and into destruction. Even the first human sin itself was not a mere mistake made by people who were hungry. After all, Adam and Eve had many trees to eat from in the garden. And it was also not about an arbitrary rule God had made. After all, that tree had been made for them, but they were not ready for it yet.

---

9 *Nephilim* is a Hebrew word for "giants." These were leaders of certain clans who were intimately associated with demonic powers that gave them knowledge and abilities beyond normal human capacity.

That first human sin was about turning away from God. He had explicitly told Adam and Eve not to eat of that tree, and yet they did it anyway. They joined the demons' rebellion against the God who had created them, loved them, and given them to each other. Indeed, He had given them the whole world so they could participate in His divine rule. In eating of the forbidden tree, they did the one thing they knew would harm and disrupt their communion with Him, and this act harmed themselves. Sin has consequences that go far beyond deliberate punishment.

Eventually, God flooded the earth to wipe it clean of demonic wickedness, in a sense "resetting" mankind by saving Noah and his family. It was only a temporary measure, however, as the problem of sin remained. As with death, God granted a system of management for sin, accepting sacrifices and prayers that temporarily cleansed sinners from their sin.

The Fall: Rule by Demons

One of my favorite tales from the Old Testament is that of the Tower of Babel. I think that may be because of my interest in language. In this narrative, found in Genesis 11:1–9, we see the whole of mankind initially speaking a single language, but by the end of the story, mankind has been divided into many languages.

In the midst of this story, which might seem to be an explanation for why there are many human languages, we see a curious episode: Humanity attempts to build a city with a tower in the middle of it, "whose top is in the heavens." I have heard this account explained as man's attempt to reach God, thinking that he can build his way to God by his own labor. The lesson is supposedly that you cannot reach God on your own; you need to be reached *by* God instead.

This explanation is not completely wrong, but it misses the point of what a tower whose top is in the heavens, placed in the center of the city, is all about.

Following the rescue of Noah and his family in Genesis 9 is another genealogy (though without the "and he died" this time), whose purpose is to enumerate the nations descended from Noah. There are seventy in all. This listing is followed in Genesis 11 by the Tower of Babel story. This story describes people who move eastward to a place called Shinar, which is traditionally where the civilization of Babylon is founded. These are the people who set about building their city and the tower in its midst.

So why build a tower to the heavens in the middle of the city? It is not out of a sense of being able literally to reach God. After all, it is not as though they saw God hovering up in the air and thought that if only they built a tall enough tower, they could get to Him. Rather, this tower is for the purpose of reaching God in a cultic sense, that is, for the purpose of worship.

Recall the ancient architecture of idolatry: a garden or temple built with an idol in the middle to trap and control the god. But when God made man, He built the worship architecture Himself and made man in His own image. So what the tower builders at Babel were doing was attempting to worship God in an idolatrous way, building their own temple and their own image of God, to sacrifice to Him the way people sacrificed to demons.

They were inverting the pattern God had set up. This inversion was therefore a rebellion against God, who warns against attempting to reach up into heaven to bring Him down (Deut.

30:12, Rom. 10:6). The tower was not a means of reaching God at all but rather of communing with and attempting to control demons. God cannot be controlled.

In this third element of the Fall, the demons' relationship to mankind is now cemented. The ziggurat (for that is what this tower was) built at Babel was designed to bring God down to man so that He would serve him. It succeeded in a sense, for God did indeed come down. He came down not to serve these idolaters but to scatter them, dividing their languages so they could not understand each other (Gen. 11:5–9).

What is not mentioned directly in Genesis 11, however, is something elucidated a bit later in the Bible, in Deuteronomy 32:8, which touches directly on this incident: "When the Most High divided their inheritance to the nations, when He separated the sons of Adam, He set the boundaries of the peoples according to the number of the angels of God."[10]

---

10 Many translations have "children of Israel" rather than "angels of God"; the latter is the reading from the Dead Sea Scrolls and Greek Septuagint. The Latin versions render this "sons of God." "Children of Israel" makes no sense, because there were more than seventy in

In other words, each of the traditional seventy nations was being assigned to an angel delegated by God as He withdrew His direct presence from the world in response to the idolatrous attempt to control Him. These angels were guardians and governors, participating in God's governance of the world. (Angels are associated not only with nations but also with the sun, moon, stars, etc.) So what happened next?

Some of the nations began to worship their angelic guardians, offering sacrifices to them. This fall into angelic idolatry is mentioned a few verses on in Deuteronomy: "They provoked Him to jealousy with foreign *gods*; / with abominations they provoked Him to anger. / They sacrificed to demons, not to God, / *to gods* they did not know, / to new *gods*, new arrivals / that your fathers did not fear" (Deut. 32:16–17 NKJV). These gods are explicitly referred to as demons in other places as well (Lev. 17:7; 2 Chr. 11:15; Ps. 106:37, etc.).[11]

Israel, these nations were not Israel, and Israel did not even exist when this division happened.

11 This fall of angels into a demonic state is actually one of five such falls described in the Bible. Contrary to some depictions of angelic falls, there is not a single "Fall" event in which all angels choose either good or evil, at least not from the point of view of humans living in

It is also worth making a linguistic point here: The word translated in Deuteronomy 32:16–17 as "demons" is *shedim*, which is not in origin a Hebrew word at all (thus standing out from the rest of the text, which is originally in Hebrew). *Shedu* (*shedim* is a Hebraized plural) is a Babylonian word referring to a territorial spirit. So these demons have territory.

This, then, is the origin of pagan idolatry, that certain angels who had been assigned by God as guardians of places and nations accepted worship from the nations, communing with them and bringing them into destruction. It is on this basis that these evil spirits are referred to as "the rulers of this age" (1 Cor. 2:6, 8) and that the Christian struggle is "against principalities, against powers, against the rulers of the darkness of this age, against spiritual *hosts* of wickedness in the heavenly *places*" (Eph. 6:12 NKJV).

So what had begun with the temptation in

---

time. For a full treatment on the five falls, see Damick, Andrew Stephen and Stephen De Young, "The Five(ish) Falls of Angels," *The Lord of Spirits* podcast on Ancient Faith Radio, Oct. 9, 2020, https://www.ancientfaith.com/podcasts/lordofspirits/the_fiveish_falls_of_angels.

Eden, bringing the introduction of death, and had been multiplied by sin, enabled by demons giving knowledge to mankind for which it was not ready, was now brought into full flower by idolatry. Idolatry had always promised to grant knowledge and abilities beyond human nature—strength, power, beauty, fertility, wealth, and so forth—but man's pursuit of these things through interaction with demons always devolved into self-worship.

This focus on the self is the reason images of these gods eventually became anthropomorphic, made to look like the humans who worshiped them. Instead of man in the image of God communing with God, gods in the image of men communed with men. And that is why this worship almost always involved sexual immorality, as well. If communing with a demon brought him into your community, then his rebellion and selfishness became sacralized and therefore would always be expressed by pursuit of the basest desires.

If it seems as if demons are involved at every step of the way when it comes to the Fall, that's because they are. In the biblical narrative, the Fall of mankind is incomprehensible without the context of the angelic rebellion that converted some angels into demons.

Many Christians or people familiar with Christianity may have a sense that angels are involved in the Christian faith but don't usually play a critical role.

But if you look closely at these core questions of why the gospel is needed, you will see that demons are central. Demons were there when death came to us, demons were there when sin multiplied, and demons were present in the dividing of the nations and the rise of pagan idolatry. Don't worry, though, because angels (that is, the ones who didn't rebel) will come into this story again later.

The enslavement of the nations to demons was the final event of the Fall. God therefore began preparing a solution. He did not choose any of the existing nations through which to make His presence known again on earth but rather formed a new nation for Himself. If you look at the list of nations in Genesis 10, you will not see this new nation listed.

This new nation is called Israel. It was formed mainly from slaves called out of Egypt but also included some Egyptians and former members of other nations. (More about these people in the next chapter.) Their emergence from Egypt is called the Exodus (detailed in the biblical book by the same name), and what formed them into a new nation is their participation in the Passover. The Passover was a sacrificial offering of a lamb which the people made to God and then ate, thus communing with Him.

Israel's purpose in the midst of the idolatrous nations was to bring God's presence to them and to intercede for them as they descended into demonic sinfulness, where the strong dominated the weak and life was held in very little regard. And finally, that mission came to fruition in producing the Messiah, Jesus Christ, who is called Emmanuel, which means "God with us." The announcement of His coming and what that means is the gospel.

So who is this Jesus?

CHAPTER 3

Who Is Jesus Christ?

When Jesus came into the region of Caesarea
Philippi, He asked His disciples, saying,
"Who do men say that I, the Son of Man,
am?" So they said, "Some say John the
Baptist, some Elijah, and others Jeremiah or
one of the prophets." He said to them, "But
who do you say that I am?" Simon Peter
answered and said, "You are the Christ, the
Son of the living God." (Matthew 16:13–16)

Before anything else we might say about Him,
we should say that Jesus is the Messiah.

He is the Messiah. He is the Christ of God.
These two words—*Messiah* and *Christ*—
came into English from Hebrew and Greek,

respectively, and they both mean "anointed one." It is a title for Jesus, not (as some might assume) His last name.

To say that Jesus is the Messiah is to import a huge history into the conversation. It is not only the history of the Israel of the Old Covenant, the People of God prior to the coming of Jesus into the world, the nation formed by God Himself through the Exodus; it is also the history of mankind and its Fall in Adam and Eve. We discussed some of that history in the preceding chapter, but we will return now to a portion of it that we have not yet mentioned.

Because of the Fall, God began a process of revealing to humanity the way out of death, sin, corruption, and enslavement to demons. He did this first through a man He chose especially for this task, Abraham.

Worshiping God or Gods?

Abraham's story begins at the end of Genesis 11, not long after the Babel story. Abraham (or Abram, as he is named at the beginning) lived in Ur, the capital of ancient Sumeria (in modern Iraq). Abram was probably there around the same time the Great Ziggurat of Ur was being constructed.

We can imagine for a moment that, as the sun set and the stars began to show themselves in the Sumerian sky, a worker building that ziggurat would have looked up at those stars. When he looked at them, he saw gods who governed the affairs of men. And as he looked upon the ziggurat sliding into darkness, he knew that after its completion the people of his civilization would stand there, offer sacrifices, and commune with their god.

And then, if he stayed a while longer, he would see moonrise. And when he looked on the moon, he saw the god to whom the ziggurat was being dedicated—Nanna, who was also called Nannar, Suen, or Sīn. Nanna was the moon god worshiped in Sumerian, Babylonian, Akkadian, and Assyrian paganism. (In many pagan myths, the moon is associated with a goddess, but Nanna is depicted as male, which is not uncommon.)

There would have been nowhere in Ur where you could not see this manmade mountain on which Nanna-idolatry would be happening. The sounds of the worship would fill the streets, and the smells of the sacrifices being burned would permeate the air. By this means, Nanna was made part of the community, and the community was inspired by this communion to imitate him and to draw strength and prosperity from him.

But the god was a demon. And he didn't want the Sumerians to prosper. He was bent on their destruction, on inspiring them to continue with him in his rebellion against God.

Abram was surrounded by idolatry, and even when his father Terah took the family and settled in Haran, Nanna was worshiped there, as well. It is in this context that in Genesis 12 God speaks to Abram, telling him to leave this place, to forsake his father's house and go to a new place that God would show him, which was called Canaan. And when he arrived in Canaan at a place called Shechem, he built an altar to God and worshiped Him by offering a sacrifice to Him (Gen. 12:1–7).

This narrative had played out before with Noah. God called Noah out from the wickedness of existing civilization, though in that case, He destroyed everything with a flood. In both cases, though, civilization is depicted ultimately as descending not from Adam but rather from Cain. It is through the line of Cain that technology came to mankind (Gen. 4:16–22), knowledge that has traditionally been held to have come via demonic involvement.[12]

Abram was thus being called out of the Cain civilization, out of involvement with demons and participation in their works, to worship God, to begin the formation of a new nation, a new civilization. In becoming the father of this nation and of many nations, Abram was renamed Abraham. He became the progenitor of Israel. And he therefore became the ancestor of Jesus Christ.

When Jesus became man, it was not the first time the Son of God had appeared to mankind. He had appeared many times before to Israel, though not by becoming human. And Israel knew Him in those previous appearances as their true God. But to understand how Jesus' coming as a man was not His first appearance on earth, and how the Son could be God while the Father

---

12 In pagan myth, this giving of secret knowledge is depicted in a positive light, such as with the Greek Prometheus giving fire or the Mesopotamian *apkallu* that gave antediluvian knowledge. But in the Christian tradition, such knowledge comes via demons (e.g., Gen. 3, or in St. Irenaeus's *On the Apostolic Preaching*, 18). Technology is not inherently demonic, but demons gave it to humans before they were ready for it, leading to their destruction.

was also God, we have to understand something about the way ancient peoples understood and interacted with divine beings.

In our time, many people believe that ancient peoples began by believing in many gods and then eventually eliminated belief in those many gods in order to believe in and worship just one God, who was seen as a single person. And then Christianity came on the scene and said that Jesus is also God, explaining that by saying there is one God who can be multiple persons at once.

But that history of religion is wrong.

For one thing, most ancient pagans did not start out worshiping many gods. Most acknowledged the existence of many gods worthy of worship but actually worshiped only one, usually regarded as local to them. The god might have a particular association, such as the Greek Athena with wisdom or the Baltic Perkunas with lightning, but the main relationship was territorial. This is called henotheism.

True polytheism in the sense of worshiping many gods came about via conquest. The gods of conquered territories were incorporated into the worship of the conquerors, who thereby hoped that the god of the territory they had conquered

would be on their side and not stir up the conquered people to rebellion against them. Pan-
theons with multiple gods assigned to various
aspects of life developed from this grouping via
conquest, and in many cases their traditional
stories merged to make them part of the same
community. In the case of empires like Rome,
the conquerors often told the locals that their
god was really the same person as a god Rome
already worshiped. The Greeks' Zeus and Arte-
mis were just different names for the Romans'
Jupiter and Diana, they said. This conflation of
worship made it easier to group gods together
in a pantheon and cement a common imperial
identity based in common worship.

So in the face of all this polytheism, what
about ancient Israel? They worshiped one God.
If you had asked a Judaean living in Jesus' time
and place how many persons he worshiped, what
would he say? If you think he would say "one,"
you would be mistaken. On the contrary, Judae-
ans of Jesus' time and place would most likely
have answered that question with "two" or sometimes "three."

How can that be possible? Isn't the Christian
doctrine of the Trinity—three divine Persons

who are one in essence—a novelty with the coming of Jesus in the first century?

To understand how ancient Israel could have worshiped multiple divine Persons yet also believed in and worshiped one God, we have to realize that such a concept—multiple persons who are all one divine being—was actually normal in the ancient world. It was normal even for pagans.

Egyptian pagans, for instance, identified their sun-god Ra as a spiritual being. And the sun in the sky was also Ra. And the pharaoh (their king) was also Ra. And the idol they worshiped in the temple was also Ra. All of these concrete manifestations were treated as Ra.

It was not as though they saw Ra as a mobile spirit who would inhabit the sun at one moment, the pharaoh the next, or the idol at another time. They did not, for instance, shut down the sacrifices in the temple when the sun was in the sky, nor did they see any contradiction with Ra being in the sky and in the idol and also in the voice of their pharaoh, all at the same time. Ra was, for them, a single being who had multiple concurrent concrete manifestations (the technical term for this is *hypostases*).

Why is this important for understanding who Jesus is? It is because ancient peoples, including Israel, were not unitarian monotheists (people who believe in and worship a god who is a single being and also a single concrete person). So when Jesus appeared on the scene in the first century, saying that He was God, and His disciples said that He was God, yet they also regarded God the Father as being "in heaven," this did not in any way contradict the idea that Israel worshiped just one God.

In fact, Israel had met Him before. He had not been invisible. They had seen God before.

The Son and Word of God

God is said to appear many times in the Old Testament: to Adam and Eve when He walked in the Garden of Eden (Gen. 3:8), to Abraham at the oak at Mamre (Gen. 18:1), and to Jacob when He wrestled with him in the night (Gen. 32:24). Prophets often saw visions of God: on His throne in heaven (Is. 6:1; Ezek. 1:26–27), or above the Ark of the Covenant (Lev. 16:2), or even speaking face to face with Moses (Ex. 33:11). One could go on and on. There was even a period when God dwelt with Israel and accompanied them visibly for more than forty years, a presence so familiar to the people that they wept when He left them (Judges 2:1–4).

These visible manifestations of God are often referred to in the Old Testament as "the Angel of the Lord" (Gen. 16:7–11; 22:11–15, et al.) or "the Word of the Lord" (Gen. 15:1–4; 1 Sam. 3:21; 15:10, et al.). The language the Old Testament uses for this figure is the language used only for Yahweh, the God of Israel, their Creator and Lord. For instance, when the Angel of the Lord appeared to Moses in the burning bush (Ex. 3:2), a few verses later the One speaking to him out of the bush is identified as God (Ex. 3:4–6).

So given all this, how is it that St. John, writing about Jesus, can write in John 1:18 that "No one has ever seen God"? Did the Apostle John simply not know about the Angel of the Lord, the Word of the Lord who is God Himself?

Sometimes when people quote John 1:18, they forget about the second half of the verse, which says, "The only[13] Son, who is in the bosom of the

---

13 The Greek *monogenes* in John 1:14 and 1:18 is translated "only-begotten" in a number of English Bibles, but there is good scholarship that points to its biblical-

Father, He has made Him known" (RSV).

This verse is actually the completion of a thought that John had been making from the beginning of the chapter. He begins by saying, "In the beginning was the Word, and the Word was with God, and the Word was God" (John 1:1). Later he says, "And the Word became flesh and dwelt among us, full of grace and truth; we have beheld his glory, glory as of the only Son from the Father" (John 1:14 RSV).

In other words, this figure who had appeared so many times in the Old Testament—this Angel of the Lord or Word of the Lord, who is indeed Yahweh, the God of Israel—is in fact the very Son of God, Jesus Christ. Saint John is referring to the existing knowledge of the appearance of God and saying that this Second Person of Yahweh whom Israel had always known is now man, and that man is Jesus Christ.

He was therefore not saying that no one had

---

era meaning as "unique" or "one and only," which is reflected in other English translations. Jesus is of course *also* the only-begotten Son of God, but that's not the point being made in John 1. The emphasis here is on the uniqueness of the Sonship of Jesus, because there are also "sons of God" who are angels.

ever seen God. He was saying that every time someone saw God, it was the Son and Word of God whom they saw. And He is now here among us. He is Jesus Christ. It is on this basis that Jesus is declared to be God in the New Testament.

The Messiah of Israel

There is something new being declared, however, and that is that the Son of God is now man. And it is the God-man Jesus Christ who is introduced as the long-expected Messiah. While that expectation derives from the very creation of mankind in Genesis, it is with Abraham that we see a clear sense that the Messiah's purpose was to save mankind from the evil that had entangled it.

God prepared the way for the Messiah by giving a way of life to Abraham's descendants (those who imitated his obedience, not only those genetically descended from him), who were called Hebrews ("wanderers") and then later Jews ("people of Judea"). Most of all, however, they were called Israel, the nation God created for Himself in the Exodus from Egypt. God spoke to this chosen people through the Prophet Moses in the Exodus and then through other prophets.

To Moses, God revealed that He was to be known to Israel as Yahweh, which means "I am" or "The One who Is" or, most literally, "The One who causes to exist" (emphasizing His role as the Creator of all things, one of the many ways He was different from the gods of the nations). The New Testament makes use of this "I am" in its Greek text. This name indicated that the way of life He was revealing was intended to enable His people to know who God is, to know their Creator not just intellectually but in a truly personal way.

This way of life revealed through Moses had one purpose: to teach Israel and the nations around them how to reconnect with God so that they could truly know Him and commune with Him (though not yet with the fullness that would come through Christ). In obeying Him and worshiping Him, they participated in Him and became more like Him, because that's what happens when you participate in worship of your god. Idolatry accomplishes the same thing, though idolaters become like their false gods—demons (see Psalms 115 and 135).

God showed Himself to Israel not only as their deity, but as their Father, which spoke of His desire for an intimate and close connection.

Over the centuries that followed Abraham and Moses, Israel was sometimes faithful to God but often lost its way.

Seeded throughout the prophecies of these men of God and growing in the tradition of Israel was the hope for the one called the Messiah, a word from Hebrew which means "anointed one." We tend to think of *messiah* as a word reserved for Jesus, but in the Old Testament, it had already been in use for some time, even aside from the specific hope for a savior figure who would rescue Israel.

Moses was a kind of messiah—a man sent from God to lead his people out of slavery in Egypt, out of the oppression of the Egyptian gods. God set him apart specifically for this task, to rouse his people out of their bondage to the Egyptian pharaoh and to bring them to the Promised Land. In Jewish tradition, the messianic hope would sometimes be expressed by comparing the Messiah to Moses. Moses is even explicitly called a "messiah" in an apocryphal text from the Dead Sea Scrolls (4Q377 Apocryphal Pentateuch).

In Leviticus 4:3, 5, *messiah* is used to refer to "the priest that is anointed." It was used not only for a particular priest but for anyone set aside for God's service. It is used for the king of Israel, especially David, whose kingly line came to be seen as particularly set apart by God.

We may remember that David is anointed by the Prophet Samuel, making him an "anointed one." But even though David and his line, established by God as kings over Israel, loom large in the messianic tradition, others are still called messiah, such as the Twelve Patriarchs or even Cyrus, the pagan ruler of the Persians whom God used to conquer Babylon and send Israel back to Jerusalem after their exile among the Babylonians.

The view of the messianic promise as the delivery from captivity and the hope of the restoration of the kingship of David developed particularly after that return from exile, when the kingship was not taken up by a descendant of David but rather by the high priests, who did not declare themselves kings but nevertheless acted as the rulers of Israel down to the time of the Maccabees. The Maccabees, who were also not descendants of David, produced the Hasmoneans, who ruled Palestine for about a century until the conquest by the Romans. The Romans, of course, set up their own client kings such as Herod, also not descended from David.

The hope remained that a deliverer would come, one who was both "the son of David" and "the Lord's anointed." We can see from the history of the use of *messiah* in the Old Testament much that prefigures Jesus, who is the Son of David, prophet, priest, king, the deliverer of captives, the One who leads His people out of the wilderness, the One who leads away from idolatry, and so forth.

The Messiah is mentioned a number of times in the Psalms and is prophesied in the Book of Daniel, where he is particularly described in terms of the restoration of Israel after return from exile in Babylon. Daniel spent his whole life in the Babylonian exile and in hope for the Messiah.

The Savior of the World

But we should not think that the messianic hope for a savior is some provincial hope confined to Israel, though it seems there were some in the time of Jesus who very much thought so. No, this hope of a redeemer, one who would restore his people, is something that extends back even to Adam and Eve and all their descendants.

The story of Israel in the Old Testament often tells the story of mankind in microcosm. We see the Exodus from Egypt and the return from the Babylonian exile, and both are images of the return of mankind from the exile from Paradise with the Fall of Adam and Eve—a restoration to the Kingdom of God.

And in both stories, we see a struggle and a purification of the people of Israel as they wandered Sinai in the Exodus or as they languished in captivity in Babylon. That is also our own story, a story of struggle and purification on the way to the Promised Land of the Kingdom of God (see 1 Cor. 10:1–12).

This is why we need to know Israel's story in the Old Testament. It is not merely the historical origins narrative of a Middle Eastern conglomeration of tribes but rather the story of mankind, both Jew and Gentile. As the Prophet Hosea's marriage to the unfaithful woman was an image of God's relationship with Israel, so is God's relationship with Israel an image of His relationship with mankind as a whole. What Israel was, mankind also was. And what Israel has become—the renewed Israel, the Church—is what mankind may also become. When the story of the Old Covenant Israel reached its fullness, the Messiah, the Anointed One of God—in Greek, *Christos*, rendered in English as *Christ*—finally was revealed.

A little over two thousand years ago, Mary, a virginal young woman who was descended from David, received a message from an archangel, one of the hosts of heaven who surround and serve God. He spoke to her of the coming of a savior who would be the Messiah and would save His people from their sins. The Holy Spirit would come upon Mary, and she would conceive the Son of God, Jesus, without any participation of an earthly father (Luke 1:26–38). The name *Jesus* means "Yahweh saves."

God had chosen Mary for this awesome task because of her purity and obedient heart. She willingly assented, saying, "Behold the maidservant of the Lord! Let it be to me according to your word" (Luke 1:38). And God also revealed to her betrothed, Joseph, the nature of this pregnancy and who the One to be born of her would be (Matt. 1:18–21).

And who is this Son of God? We have already

said many things about Him, but here is a summary of who He is: He is both divine and human, both fully God and fully man. He is the second Person of the Holy Trinity, which consists of Father, Son, and Holy Spirit. He is human in every way yet without sin. He is one divine Person in two natures—divine and human.

With the Incarnation—a word that means "taking on flesh," indicating that God has now truly become man—humanity is now joined to God.

The Life of Jesus

When Jesus was born in Bethlehem of Judea (a city in Israel, the city of David), His coming was announced: angels appeared to shepherds nearby (Luke 2:8–20), and a star appeared to wise men in the East (probably Persia), who journeyed from there to find Him (Matt. 2:1–12).

Jesus grew up just as any human boy does. At the age of thirty, He approached St. John the Baptist (also called John the Forerunner) at the Jordan River and was baptized there by him—He was immersed in the water and came out again. At this event, St. John said of Him, "Behold!

The Lamb of God who takes away the sin of the world!" (John 1:29).

Jesus' baptism began His mission of sanctifying all creation, driving out the demons, and reestablishing the rule of God (we'll go into more detail on that in chapter 4). During His three years of public ministry on Earth, He not only taught the commandments of God but also healed people of their sickness, both spiritual and physical. Jesus particularly focused His ministry on twelve disciples, who were mostly drawn from the laboring classes, especially fishermen. As His mission drew to a close, one of His disciples, named Judas Iscariot, betrayed Him and handed Him over to the local Jewish authorities. In turn, they gave Him over to the Roman imperial authorities, who crucified Him by the authority of the governor, Pontius Pilate. Jesus was legally convicted as a blasphemer against Jewish law.

The penalty of crucifixion—being nailed to a large wooden cross and hung there to suffocate to death—was used by the Romans to execute the lowest people in society, the worst of the *non personae*. It may seem odd that the Romans would even care if someone blasphemed against

Jewish law (they regarded non-Romans as basically equivalent to livestock and cared nothing for their customs), but their prime concern was keeping the peace. Since they had reason to believe that Jesus would be the occasion of a riot, it made sense to execute Him. It was easier to stop a riot by executing one man than to keep the peace by massacring the locals (which they often did).

Jesus died on a Friday, the day before Israel's greatest annual holy day, the Passover—a day that commemorated their delivery from slavery in Egypt and that formed them as a people. Jesus rose from the dead on the third day, Sunday. Through this voluntary death and resurrection, Jesus broke the power of death over all mankind forever, becoming Himself the fulfillment of the Passover.

After His resurrection, He was seen alive by many, including the eleven disciples (Judas, in his remorse over betraying Christ, had already committed suicide) and many others. He spent another forty days on Earth, further instructing His eleven disciples in order to equip them as *apostles*, a word which means "those sent out on a mission." After those forty days, He physically ascended into heaven while the apostles watched.

So when we say that Jesus is the Messiah and the Savior of the world, this is what we mean. We mean that He is the hope not only of Old Testament Israel but of all mankind. Israel as the chosen people of God in the Old Covenant served to provide the image for the narrative that defined all of humanity. Jesus is the Messiah of Israel—the Christ—the One who would redeem them, the Son of David who would lead them out of exile, the Anointed One who would restore kingship and priesthood to Israel. He is not only the Son of David but the Son of God, and so He is the Messiah not only of the Old Covenant Israel but also of the renewed Israel, the Church, the New Covenant into which all mankind is invited, including the Jews. He has led us all out of bondage in the Egypt of our sin, out of exile in the Babylon of our passions, out of idolatry to anything we worship except Him.

When we say that Jesus is the Messiah, we assume all this Old Testament background and what He did in the New Testament. If we do not know it, then it makes no sense to call Him Messiah. It makes no sense to call Him the Anointed One if we do not know what the purpose is for which He was anointed. It makes no sense to call the Church the New Israel if we know nothing about the Old Israel.

As we learn the gospel, we do not necessarily have to have all this history memorized—and there is a great deal more to know, too! But we do need to know that Jesus as the Messiah is the Anointed One who was sent from God to lead His people out of slavery, exile, and idolatry, to restore and perfect kingship and priesthood, to defeat demonic oppression. He is the fulfillment of all the prophecy of the Old Testament, the culmination of the hopes not only of the Jews but of all mankind since Adam and Eve.

Thus having been introduced to who He is, we may rightly ask, what did He accomplish?

CHAPTER 4

What Did Jesus Christ Accomplish?

O Death, where is your sting?
O Hell, where is your victory?
Christ is risen, and you are overthrown!
Christ is risen, and the demons are fallen!
Christ is risen, and the angels rejoice!
Christ is risen, and life reigns!
Christ is risen, and not one dead
remains in the grave!
(Paschal Homily of St. John Chrysostom)

We saw in chapter 2 why the gospel was needed at all, with the three problems that make up the Fall: death, sin, and rule by demons. All three were managed but not defeated under the Old Covenant. In the New Covenant, what Jesus Christ accomplished was to defeat all three of these problems, though roughly in reverse order.

Before we get into the details, however, it is critical that we understand this: Christ's mission is a mission of love. No pagan god ever loved his worshipers. The gospel announcement was thus profoundly astonishing and revolutionary to the ancient world: that the God of the cosmos, the God of gods, the Lord of lords, the Lord of hosts, would reach out in love to lowly human beings— including women, children, and slaves, whom the ancient world saw as not fully human—and rescue them from demons, sin, and death.

It is within this frame of the self-sacrificing love of God that we now will examine the three accomplishments of Christ that are key to the gospel.

Undoing the Fall: Exorcism

In the aftermath of Babel, mankind was subjected to rule by demons, expressed and reinforced especially through idolatry, the worship of fallen angels. Participating in demonic activity puts you in communion with demons, and that makes you more like them.

The most obvious way to participate with demons is through idolatry, in which sacrifices are offered to demons, then eaten by worshipers. This shared meal is an act of communion, which makes the demon part of your community and gives him influence over your life. No Christian in the ancient world regarded these rituals as fake. They understood that they worked. They put you in communion with your god.

This dynamic also works even through less obviously "religious" worship, that is, by sacrificing to the passions that are always inflamed through demonic activity. So, while someone of our own day might not be offering up animal or other food sacrifices to Aphrodite, he might be sacrificing his time, possessions, relationships, and so forth in pursuit of physical beauty. Or he might not worship Loki, but he will make sacrifices in his life to torment others. Other sacrifices might be to gluttony, wrath, power, and so on. Such sacrifices have an effect similar to that of putting a slaughtered bull on an altar to Zeus.

Likewise, any sinful activity is participation

with demons: "He who sins is of the devil, for the devil has sinned from the beginning" (1 John 3:8a). And even one's desires are bound up with the devil if one is associated with him (John 8:44).

Under the Old Covenant, the domination of the nations by demons was managed by the creation of a new nation, Israel. But that did not end the problem, for Israel was tempted to idolatry many times and fell into it. The demons had to be driven out once and for all.

We can therefore see why a major aspect of Jesus' ministry was exorcism, the casting out of demons: "For this purpose the Son of God was manifested, that He might destroy the works of the devil" (1 John 3:8b). Destroying the devil's works is not just one of the things Jesus did, but is the very purpose of His manifestation on earth.

Therefore, the exorcisms Jesus performed in His time on earth were not a mere sideshow to demonstrate His power or an *ad hoc* fix for people's bodily ailments. Driving out demons was core to His mission. He had come to reclaim the world for God's Kingdom, so it makes sense that He would spend time driving out the oppressors and false rulers.

One of the major themes we see in Jesus' mission of exorcism is that people often are healed of sicknesses at the same time. By casting out demons, Jesus cured insanity (Luke 8:26–37), seizures (Matt. 17:14–21), blindness and muteness (Matt. 12:22–32), and so forth. Why is physical health so connected with exorcism? It is because all evils in the world were understood to be bound up with demonic activity. That does not mean that everyone who is ill is "possessed" by a demon or has committed some great sin, but it does mean that sickness is associated with demons.

Perhaps most interestingly in terms of exorcism, we should recall the baptism of Jesus by St. John the Forerunner. Traditional Christian iconography of that scene shows water gods in the river beneath Jesus' feet—usually little figures riding on fish or sea monsters, and there are often draconic or serpentine creatures being crushed beneath His feet. The point here is that He was overcoming the chaos of the whole creation that is associated with these false gods. In other words, the exorcism ministry of Jesus was cosmic in scope. Demons had to be destroyed and driven out, not just from people but from creation itself.

Undoing the Fall: Forgiveness of Sin

As we have seen, in Jesus' time sin was regarded as the work of the devil or other demons. This understanding contrasts with the modern view some Christians have, which tends to see sin as mainly a transgression of a law. If sin is seen solely as law-breaking, then it is a crime deserving a punishment. Thus, sin is dealt with by legal penalties. Within that model, what Jesus accomplished was to take the penalty for sin on Himself so that Christians would not be punished.

That view of Christ as the substitute for mankind may not be entirely wrong, but it is only a small part of the story. The problem with sin is not that sinners have a black mark against them. It is that they have been transformed by sin into people who are involved with demons. They imitate demons because they are in communion with them. And that applies not only to certain great sinners but to every sinner, which means every person.

Being an existential problem rather than merely a legal one, sin therefore is a kind of sickness and even addiction. That means that forgiveness of sins involves changing the human person into someone who is in communion with God and in the process of becoming like Him instead of what results from demonic communion.

Under the Old Covenant, sin was managed through the system of sacrifices and purifications given in the Levitical law. The priests offered sacrifices of animals and other food as well as practicing purification with blood and ashes, centered especially on the ritual of the Day of Atonement. These actions cleansed Israel from sin but did not end sin.

Christ's accomplishment was to destroy the power of sin by giving true, permanent cleansing through the offering of His own blood on the cross and through His resurrection. This forgiveness is received initially through Christian baptism, given in the likeness of the Flood of Noah (1 Pet. 3:20–21). And when Christians fall into sin again, it can be forgiven through confession (John 20:23; 1 John 1:9) and through the Eucharist (Matt. 26:26–28).

Undoing the Fall: Resurrection

The mission of Christ in this world to establish the Kingdom and to defeat and drive out His enemies is finally completed in His destruction of the last enemy, which is death itself: "Then *comes* the end, when He delivers the kingdom to God the Father, when He puts an end to all rule and all authority and power. For He must reign till He has put all enemies under His feet. The last enemy *that* will be destroyed *is* death" (1 Cor. 15:24–26 NKJV).

The resurrection is absolutely critical to Christianity because it is the full and final triumph of Jesus Christ. It is what makes Christianity what it is. It is the very heart of the gospel.

To understand the full meaning of the resurrection, we have to look more closely at who Jesus is and how that fits into what it means that He rose from the dead. Christianity is unique in this claim: God became truly man, truly died, and then truly rose bodily from the grave. No other religion makes this claim about itself. No one else dares to say that the God-man has died and come back to life.

Now one may quibble: Are there not ancient pagan gods who became man? There are many who appeared in the *form* of humans, to be sure. But those same gods were often just as likely to appear as bulls or snakes or cats. No one ever said that they *became* man in the sense of truly having human nature while also retaining the nature of God. Gods were one thing, and mortals were another. A god might appear to be a man, but he didn't become one. The best you get is an avatar, a god in the shape of a man, or a demi-god, a kind of half-god, half-man.

Jesus Christ is unique among all claims to deity in that He claims to be the Son of God, truly God in all things, who became the Son of Mary, truly human in all things. That anyone ever claimed such a thing is kind of crazy, given this prior background—that gods would not lower themselves to become human. And it only seemed crazier once pagan philosophers started positing a single, omnipotent creator-god. Once they agreed on the existence of a god so far outside of time and space that he no longer resembled the petty pagan gods, the idea that he would come among us as truly man was even more unthinkable. The religious trend in the first century was not to make deity seem more like humanity. On the contrary, religion was beginning to dehumanize God.

One may also quibble: Were there not ancient pagan gods who died and then came back to life?

In the nineteenth century, the category of the "dying and rising god" came to be much discussed in scholarly circles. Many names were put forward—the Semitic Baal; the Greek Adonis, Dionysius, and Persephone; the Egyptian Ra and Osiris; the Akkadian Ishtar; and the Korean Bari. But most pagan gods that die do not rise again. And most who do rise again do not rise as the same deity but are transformed into someone else in some way. Furthermore, none of those dying gods even claimed to be God in the sense that the God of Abraham, Isaac, and Jacob is God. None of them are the one, true God who is the reason that existence exists, the One who sustains reality by His power, the One who created all things, is above all things, is outside all things and yet within all things. That kind of god doesn't get proposed by pagans until later.

And when that kind of god did get proposed by Greek philosophy, the idea that he could die would not have made sense to anyone. If all of existence depended on "the One," the Unmoved Mover, then how could that One ever die? Death has no meaning in that philosophical world of uncreated deity, in which the true God does not contemplate anything but himself. In that model, even creation has to be accomplished by a separate divine being called the demiurge.

So while in the nineteenth and twentieth centuries scholars played around with the idea that Jesus was just one god among many who died and rose again, reading those pagan stories in their integrity shows that none of them actually made the claim that Christians make about Jesus. Jesus is the one true God become truly human who truly dies and then truly rises from the dead. Even non-Christian scholars have basically abandoned the argument of His non-uniqueness, though of course it still gets currency in popular media and on the Internet.

When Christians say "Christ is risen," it is not just some provincial variant on a universal religious theme. We are daring to say something never said before. None of the religions that followed the rise of the Church have dared to say the same thing. They all backed off in one way or another—usually in terms of the true deity of Jesus or His true humanity. They simply couldn't bring themselves to say that the one true God became true man, truly died, and then truly rose.

It's critical that we understand the uniqueness of the traditional Christian message about the death and resurrection of Jesus. This is why, when the gospel message was first preached, most people found it unbelievable—it was preposterous, like nothing they'd ever heard before. And even now, it is unbelievable to most people for exactly the same reason. That God could truly become man, that there could be a resurrection from the dead, and that said resurrection should begin with the God-man seems crazy to most people these days—sometimes even to Christian people.

Someone once told me about an exchange he had with his teenaged niece in Paris. She had been raised as a devout Methodist in the southern United States. They were attending Easter Mass at Notre Dame Cathedral. His niece turned to him and said, "Where is Jesus' body?"

He replied, "He rose from the dead."

She said, "Yes, but what happened to His body?"

It turned out that this young lady, raised a pious churchgoer her whole life, believed that Jesus' soul had been raised but that His body was left behind somewhere. And she wanted to know where they kept it.

When Jesus rose from the dead, it wasn't some ethereal "spiritual" experience. We mean that the heart that had stopped beating began pumping blood again, that the soul that had descended into Hades was put back in His body, that the lungs that had stopped breathing air suddenly inhaled once again. The God-man who had nails stuck through His hands and feet and a spear stuck into His side, who cried out with a loud voice, bowed His head, and then gave up His spirit—that God-man who had been crucified like a thief walked out of His tomb on the two legs that had formed when He was growing in the womb of His mother, the Virgin Mary. His resurrected body functioned differently than before, for sure, but it was still His own body, and He was still the same Jesus. And the tomb is empty.

When Christians say that Christ is risen, we should say it so clearly that people will laugh at the idea because it's crazy. It should sound crazy to people. It should sound just as freaky as the idea of a body lying in the coffin at a funeral suddenly getting up, throwing all the stuff people put into coffins out on the floor, and asking for a hand to climb out.

And this is no zombie-life, either, no undeath in which a mindless, moaning body animated by some evil force goes wandering about in search of brains to munch on. No, this is life in its truest, fullest sense, a life you could see in His eyes and in His smile, in His speech, in the fact that He ate fish and bread and even honeycomb for dessert.

He's alive! Christ is risen, and this changes everything.

If it were not enough that we make the crazy claim that God became man and that the God-man died, now we are talking about someone who is dead getting up and being *not dead*. This is not normal.

This gospel is no denatured little bit of spiritual comfort that makes us feel good. This gospel is the God who created all things blasting His way into our reality, smashing up death, and wiping out its power.

Christ is risen, and death is slain: "O Death, where *is* your sting? / O Hades, where *is* your victory?" (1 Cor. 15:55 NKJV).

As the Apostle Peter stood up on the Day of Pentecost and said, "Therefore let all the house of Israel know assuredly that God has made this Jesus, whom you crucified, both Lord and Christ" (Acts 2:36): this Jesus, whose "soul was not left in Hades, nor did His flesh see corruption. This Jesus God has raised up, of which we are all witnesses" (2:31–32).

This gospel of the resurrection was so powerful that all but one of the twelve apostles were killed for teaching it, because the message excluded the worship of the Roman gods on which the empire was built and declared the advent of a new Kingdom. The apostles voluntarily went to their deaths proclaiming that they had seen Jesus risen, that they would preach the resurrection no matter what happened, that they would obey God rather than men (Acts 5:29), that they would stand in the temple and in the synagogues and in the streets and travel to the corners of the earth to speak all the words of this Life (Acts 5:20).

Our God is not dead! they said. *He's alive!*

One of the most magnificent summaries of the resurrection of Jesus Christ is found in the anaphora of St. Basil the Great, the core of his Divine Liturgy text, which the Orthodox Church uses for eucharistic worship:

He gave Himself a ransom to Death, whereby we were held, sold into bondage under sin.

And having descended into Hades through the Cross, that He might fill all things with Himself, He loosed the pains of death, and rose again on the third day, making a way for all flesh unto the resurrection from the dead, for it was not possible that the Author of life should be held by corruption, that He might be the First-fruits of those who have fallen asleep, the First-born from the dead, that He might be in all things the first among all.

That sermon of St. Peter at Pentecost is reflected there in St. Basil's words, along with words from St. Paul (1 Cor. 15:20; Col. 1:18) and St. John (Rev. 1:5).

The Apostle Paul put it this way:

But if there is no resurrection of the dead, then Christ is not risen. And if Christ is not risen, then our preaching is empty and your faith is also empty. Yes, and we are found false witnesses of God, because we have testified of God that He raised up Christ, whom He did not raise up—if in fact the dead do not rise. For if the dead do not rise, then Christ is not risen. And if Christ is not risen, your faith is futile; you are still in your sins! Then also those who have fallen asleep in Christ have perished. If in this life only we have hope in Christ, we are of all men the most pitiable. (1 Cor. 15:13–19 NKJV)

But there *is* resurrection from the dead. Christ *is* risen. This is the final accomplishment of Jesus—to defeat His last enemy, which is death.

What is the takeaway here? The work of Jesus was about establishing the Kingdom of God, which meant defeating three enemies—the demons who dominate the nations, the sin that infects and addicts mankind, and finally, death itself.

The moment of Christ's resurrection is referred to in Greek as the *Anastasis*—the Arising. It is more than resurrection in the sense of rising as from sleep. The Greek word for this is *egersis*, which is also used to refer to resurrection in the Bible. *Anastasis* refers to standing up or coming to attention. It is an aggressive, almost military term. We might even translate it as *uprising*.

If we understand Christ's defeat of death correctly in light of all that we have just said, then we know that the Arising is not simply a metaphysical victory ending the physical effect of death. Rather, the defeat of death is the destruction of the last power of Christ's enemies the demons. It is in this context that we read of the Arising in Psalm 82:6–8 (RSV):

> *I say, "You are gods,*
> *sons of the Most High, all of you;*
> *nevertheless, you shall die like men,*
> *and fall like any prince."*

> *Arise, O God, judge the earth;*
> *for to thee belong all the nations!*

Here we see God, having stood up to judge the gods (82:1), rendering justice upon those sons of the Most High who rebelled against Him. They "shall die like men, and fall like any prince" because they afflicted mankind (82:2–5).

Finally, this prophecy given centuries before Christ's birth says that His resurrection—the Arising—will bring judgment to the earth and will return to Him the authority over the nations that had been abused by the demons: "Arise, O God, judge the earth; for to thee belong all the nations!"

The moment of Christ's resurrection is therefore the moment when the doom of the dark powers is sealed. It was the decisive moment that turned the tide of the war. Christ now rules in the midst of His enemies (Ps. 110:2). He has defeated them, and they are routed, but in their retreat they rage and seek to draw as many of us as possible into destruction with them.

When Christians say "Christ is risen!" we are openly declaring our allegiance to the Victor in this war of reconquest by preaching how Jesus has defeated His enemies. The gospel therefore contains at its very heart an act of spiritual warfare.

We have now seen the first two of the elements of the gospel of Jesus Christ: Who is Jesus? What did He accomplish? He has been announced by His heralds the apostles and prophets, and He is proclaimed as greater than even Caesar Augustus and a conqueror who can defeat death itself.

So given who He is and what He has done, what does He expect of those who hear this gospel?

CHAPTER 5

What Does Jesus Christ Expect of Us?

For this is the love of God, that we keep His commandments. And His commandments are not burdensome. (1 John 5:3)

We have discussed in some detail the beloved, now-Christian term *evangelion* in its pre-Christian sense and how that frames the Christian gospel, noting that an evangelion has three constituent pieces—who the coming ruler is, what he has accomplished, and what he expects of those who hear the gospel. We turn now to this final portion of the content of the gospel.

This final piece may be illumined by another word that we now think of as essentially Christian: *kerygma*. It's not as familiar to most as *gospel*, but it is nonetheless a key term in the core of Christian theology. *Kerygma* in Christian theology refers to the proclamation of the gospel. It is the content of the preaching. It has also come to be understood as the core public proclamation of the gospel and is therefore in some sense synonymous with *gospel*.

But before *kerygma* took on this narrow technical sense within Christianity, it had a pre-Christian usage and, like *evangelion*, it had a public and even imperial sense. The word *kerygma* itself comes from the verb *kerysso*, which means "to proclaim publicly." And the noun *keryx* denotes the person who does this proclaiming, synonymous with the English *herald*. Thus the kerygma is that spoken by the keryx. Saint Paul uses these terms many times to refer to what his task is as an apostle.

If a keryx rode into your town and proclaimed a kerygma to you, it wasn't just the evening news. Because it was a specifically *public* proclamation, it usually implied a call to action, even a summons. You were expected to do something as a result of receiving the kerygma.

A kerygma might be military orders from a commander. You might be getting your marching orders or a summons to military service. You might be summoned to appear before the emperor or invited to attend a public debate between philosophers. Whatever its specific content, the key here is that a kerygma is not just a piece of information, a message from one person to another, but it is rather specifically a *public* proclamation, which meant that it had implications for the whole community.

The public character of the gospel contrasts with the way many religions in the first century were transmitted, that is, as secret wisdom given only to a few worthy people. The gospel was a kerygma and therefore not esoteric knowledge whispered by priests to their most devoted followers, cryptically encoded into obscure and difficult texts and hidden ritual. The gospel proclaimed the coming of the King of kings, whose rule was extending throughout the whole cosmos, and so it was proclaimed openly. And everyone was expected to respond. Everyone was offered citizenship in this coming kingdom.

The public character of this proclamation also

contrasts with the distorted modern sense of the gospel being a kind of sales pitch. Why? Because it means that the Kingdom is coming whether we want it to or not. The question is not whether each of us finds the Kingdom appealing or suited to our religious tastes, but rather whether we will be part of it or not.

Jesus Christ has defeated the demons, sin, and death, but why do they all still afflict us? It is because that conquest has not yet come to its fullness. Christ is already reigning here on earth as King, but "He must reign till He has put all enemies under His feet" (1 Cor. 15:25). He is ruling in the midst of His enemies (Ps. 110:2).

His Kingdom has come, is coming, and is also not yet fully manifest. The Scripture uses this language, saying that the Kingdom has already come (Matt. 12:28), is "at hand" (Matt. 3:10), and is also yet to come (Matt. 6:10). And that means that we still have a choice of whether to align ourselves with Him or with His enemies.

So what do we have to do to be part of this Kingdom? How do we align ourselves with Christ? What is it that the heralded King expects of us?

The Covenant of Faithfulness with God

The foundation for understanding what God expects of us lies again in the Old Testament. The key term for it is *covenant* (in Hebrew, *berith,* and in Greek, *diathiki*). This word is used many times throughout the Scripture, and all instances of it are instructive for us. But let's look particularly at the covenant given to Israel through Moses, because that is the covenant on which the gospel covenant is based and which is fulfilled by it.

Like *gospel, covenant* is a concept that existed in the ancient world and gets used by the biblical writers to express the arrangement God made with Israel. We will discuss both the Ten Commandments and also some passages from Deuteronomy and others later, but the context for these is the ancient suzerainty treaty. By such treaties, a newly ascendant king would make an agreement with his vassals, with consequences for both obedience and disobedience.

A copy of the treaty would be set at the foot of the king's throne to remind him of his promises, and another copy would be set next to the idol of the god worshiped by the community, to recruit the god as a witness. In the context of Israel, the tablets of the covenant were placed at the Ark of the Covenant—simultaneously the footstool of the throne of God and the place where He was worshiped. The king of Israel, once one was appointed, was later instructed to make a copy for himself, as well.

This covenant is referred to as the Old Covenant,[14] distinguishing it from the New Covenant in Christ. The Old Covenant is also sometimes referred to simply as *the Law* (in Hebrew, the *Torah*) or sometimes *the Law and the Prophets*. The distinction does not mean, however, that the latter replaces the former. Rather, the New Covenant is the *fulfillment* of the Old Covenant. In the period of the Old Covenant, it was referred to simply as *the covenant*, but some of the prophets, such as Joel, Jeremiah, and Ezekiel, predicted the coming of a new covenant. All is thus fulfilled in Christ and with His sending of the Holy Spirit at Pentecost (Acts 1).

---

14 In most languages, *Old Covenant* and *Old Testament* are the same words (and the same is true for *New Covenant* and *New Testament*), but in English, we have come to use *covenant* in these phrases to refer to the relationship with God and *testament* to refer to the collection of biblical texts.

This language of fulfillment is used by Christ Himself: "Do not think that I came to destroy the Law or the Prophets. I did not come to destroy but to fulfill" (Matt. 5:17). People sometimes read that to mean, effectively, "I did not come to destroy but really I came to destroy." But *fulfill* does not mean *destroy*. There is certainly change and even transformation, but not abolition.

Why is this important? It means that if we are to understand the New Covenant, the Old Covenant is still very much relevant. *Fulfillment* rather than *destruction* means that God hasn't changed His mind about what He expects of those in His Kingdom. The Old Covenant is still in force, but it has been filled to the full in the New.

We will not go here into all the details of the relationship between the Old and New Covenants, but for our purposes, it suffices to say that in the kerygma proclaimed by the Apostles of Christ, there is no sense in which what came before them is now abolished. Instead, it is transformed into something superior because of the coming of Christ.

Running as a common thread between the Old and New Covenants is the covenant made with Abraham, in which God promised to him that his descendants would be both as numerous as the sands of the sea and also blessed like the stars in the sky (Gen. 15:5; 22:17). What does that mean? Ancient peoples understood the stars to be closely associated with angelic beings, so much so that in some cases, pagans would worship them (Deut. 4:19). God is promising Abraham that his descendants will be like angelic beings.

And who are Abraham's descendants? Are they people who can trace their genealogy back to him? No, it is only those who are faithful to God who are counted as Abraham's heirs (Gal. 3:7). Even in the formation of Israel in Exodus, people who were not genealogically descended from Abraham were included because of their faithfulness. Again and again, the Scriptures attest to faithfulness being what makes someone part of God's righteous covenant: "The just shall live by faithfulness" (Hab. 2:4; Rom. 1:17; Gal. 3:11; etc.).[15]

---

15 In nearly all English Bibles, the word *faith* (in Greek, *pistis*) appears in these and related passages, but this translation is the result of an attempt to appeal to Protestant theology, which centers on belief rather than action. It is clear from context, however, and

But isn't being part of the covenant about "having faith" or simply believing? No, it requires continuous action and loyalty. As Christ said, "Not everyone who says to Me, 'Lord, Lord,' shall enter the kingdom of heaven, but he who does the will of My Father in heaven" (Matt. 7:21). He also said, "He who endures to the end will be saved" (Matt. 10:22; 24:13; Mark 13:13).

It is not faithfulness that keeps us in God's covenant—we cannot achieve even that without His help. But it is *through* our faithfulness that God's work in us is accomplished (Eph. 2:8). Thus, anyone can become an heir of the promises to Abraham if he is faithful like Abraham.

Switching Sides

Life in God's covenant means faithfulness to Him. But that is not a neutral course of action, nor is it one that goes unopposed. If we keep faith with God, then we *break faith* with the

---

even grammatically that the translation ought to be *faithfulness*, which implies action. Likewise, the word usually translated *believe* is the same Greek word as the one that gets translated *have faith*, and it means *be faithful*. The word usually translated *believers* is properly translated *the faithful*.

other side in the war that was launched by the rebellious angelic beings. And there are no civilians or bystanders in this war. There is no neutral ground. Thus, we see that paying heed to the kerygma means that we are choosing a side and answering the call to fight. Choosing a side means not only standing with the army to which you pledge your allegiance but also actively participating in that side's combat. Civilians in human war may try to stay out of harm's way, but in the spiritual war, the battle front is everywhere, so there are no civilians. Everyone has to take up arms. You take up arms against the other side by joining your comrades and doing what they do. But if you fight against your comrades, it's clear which side you're on. Saint John the Apostle describes this conflict in terms of sin and righteousness:

> Whoever commits sin also commits lawlessness, and sin is lawlessness. And you know that He was manifested to take away our sins, and in Him there is no sin. Whoever abides in Him does not sin. Whoever sins has neither seen Him nor known Him. Little children, let no one deceive you. He who

practices righteousness is righteous, just as He is righteous. He who sins is of the devil, for the devil has sinned from the beginning. For this purpose the Son of God was manifested, that He might destroy the works of the devil. Whoever has been born of God does not sin, for His seed remains in him; and he cannot sin, because he has been born of God. In this the children of God and the children of the devil are manifest: Whoever does not practice righteousness is not of God, nor is he who does not love his brother. (1 John 3:4–10 NKJV)

Here St. John tells us that sin shows someone to be "of the devil." That is, sin shows which side we're on, and it's the side of the demons who, as we saw in chapter 2, exercise dominion over us. Yet the Son of God came to Earth "that He might destroy the works of the devil," as we saw in chapter 4. So the two sides in the spiritual war are defined by sin (for the demons) and righteousness (for God).

We can do either the works of the devil, showing us to be his "children," or the works of God, showing us to be His children instead. It is a common thread throughout the Scriptures that being someone's son or offspring means doing his works, imitating him, participating in his life. So we have a choice between participating in the life of God or in the pseudo-life of the demons.

The gospel therefore includes the expectation that those who hear it will switch sides, abandoning the army of the devil and all the demons and pledging new allegiance to the Son of God, who came to destroy the works of demons. We switch sides by abandoning sin and doing works of righteousness.

Repentance: Abandoning the Demonic

The most common gospel proclamation in Scripture is quite brief: "Repent, for the kingdom of heaven is at hand." This message was preached both by Jesus Christ Himself (Matt. 4:17) and by St. John the Forerunner before Him (Matt. 3:2). Repentance is the means by which we switch sides in the war. So how do we do that?

To turn from sin to righteousness is not merely a matter of ceasing to do bad things. Sin is fundamentally a kind of demonic force that masters us and makes us demonic slaves when we give in to it (John 8:34). Righteousness, therefore, is freedom from slavery to sin, but it also means commitment to a new master (Rom. 6:18). You cannot switch sides in this war without actually enlisting on the side of God and obeying His marching orders.

Obedience to God's commandments includes a number of "don'ts," such as the several prohibitions in the Ten Commandments (Ex. 20:1–17)—those against idolatry, taking oaths by God's name, murder, adultery, theft, lying, and envy. Someone who does these things and does not repent of them is participating with demons and rejoining their rebellion. (That same set of commandments from God also includes "dos"—worship of God and honor for parents. We will discuss these and others further on.)

But God's commands for how to be obedient to Him are not exhausted by the commandments in Exodus 20. He also forbids all sexual immorality, which is linked almost everywhere in the Scriptures with idolatry. And why? As we saw above, idolatry is about pleasing yourself by attempting to control demons rather than being obedient to God. And all forms of sexual immorality are idolatrous. God proclaimed that sexual relationships are blessed only within marriage between a man and a woman. To stray from that is to follow our own desires and not His.

And even though our era in history has picked certain forms of sexual immorality and declared them blameless, God lists acts of fornication, adultery, incest, homosexuality, and bestiality all in the same category in Leviticus 18. He also identifies such behavior with the pagans who lived in the land where Israel resided, saying it was for this reason that the land was "defiled" and "vomited them out" (17:24–28).

I know this commandment is hard to hear in our day, but to be Christian, obedient to God, on His side in the war, requires we stop following our own selfish desires and start following Christ's desires for us (Mark 8:34–35). Repentance does not mean we will stop feeling these desires. It means we now follow our new Master, with His help mastering ourselves, not pursuing everything we desire just because we desire it, even if we desire it very deeply. It is not only sexual immorality that constitutes a return to the demonic army. Oppressing the weak and the poor is likewise demonic. God said He will come to vindicate those whom the rich and powerful oppress. The Day of the Lord (referenced in numerous places in the Bible) will see God bringing His justice to the Earth, meaning that He will make things right, lifting up the fallen and bringing low the proud and unmerciful.

To repent, therefore, is to turn away from these demonic ways of living, to stop participating in demonic works, and to participate instead in the works of God. The Greek word used in Scripture for repentance is *metanoia*, and it means a "turning of the mind." It means to set our minds on God and to do what is good and not what is evil. So what is the good?

Repentance: Joining with the Angelic

As we saw earlier, God says to the rebellious angels in His judgment of them, "How long will you judge unjustly / and show partiality to the wicked? / Give justice to the weak and the fatherless; / maintain the right of the afflicted and the destitute. / Rescue the weak and the needy; / deliver them from the hand of the wicked" (Psalm 82:2–4 RSV). We see how the demons are judged by God for not fulfilling their assigned angelic role, which is what it means to live demonically. But we also see what it means to live angelically.

Christ's expectation for us is that we follow the law of love rather than that of selfishness. We will receive the benefits of God's blessings in the covenant if we love and obey Him: "Therefore know that the LORD your God, He *is* God, the faithful God who keeps covenant and mercy for a thousand generations with those who love Him and keep His commandments" (Deut. 7:9 NKJV). That does not mean that God does not love us if we don't love and obey Him—Christ died for us even while we were yet sinners (Rom. 5:8)—but if we remain in rebellion against Him, we do not receive the benefits of the covenant with the God who is love.

Doing the works of God means being like Him, and He has revealed Himself as love: "And we have known and believed the love that God has for us. God is love, and he who abides in love abides in God, and God in him" (1 John 4:16). Instead of abiding in demons, by love we abide in God. Those same commandments given to Israel included the commands to worship God and to honor one's parents. God alone receives worship and our deepest love, but our fellow human beings receive honor and loving care from us. This same dynamic appears elsewhere in Scripture: "Honor all *people*. Love the brotherhood. Fear God. Honor the king" (1 Pet. 2:17). Also: "You shall love the LORD your God with all your heart, with all your soul, with all your strength, and with all your mind, and your neighbor as yourself" (Deut. 6:5; Luke 10:27).

Above all, to love God means to worship Him. Worship in Scripture is centered on sacrifice. And what is sacrifice? It is not about killing animals or merely about giving something up. Not all Old Covenant sacrifices involved animals (some included drink, wheat cakes, etc.), and a thing can be given up without making a sacrifice. The clue is that sacrifices were always in the form of food. To sacrifice is to share a meal with your god. All ancient religions practiced this. Food was set on an altar before the god. Part of it was given to him, part to the priests, and part to the people.[16] In offering and eating of the sacrifice, therefore, people gave hospitality to their god and came into communion with him. The

---

16 There are other kinds of sacrifices, too, such as whole-burnt offerings and incense, but that is outside my point here. These nonetheless serve a similar function, though it is more about purification by means of contact with God.

god's community merged with the people's.

In the sacrifice offered by Christ and given to Christians—the Eucharist—He is offering hospitality to us and making us part of His own family. The Eucharist is the very heart of the New Covenant and forms the basis of our relationship with God.[17] We thus become "sons of God, equal to the angels" (Luke 20:36)[18] who are part of His royal household. Loving God means, above all else, devotion to worship, but also to prayer, to almsgiving, to praising Him, to seeking Him in all parts of our life, dedicating all of it to Him.

We are likewise called to love and honor other people. If the demons seek to destroy and to pit humans against one another, God's faithful angelic beings do the opposite. They build up, reconcile, and unite. We are called in the gospel to live as they do. Angels were given reign over the creation to help maintain and develop it, and they were given guardianship over human beings to watch over them, care for them, and draw them to God. Human beings faithful to God's

---

17 Matt. 26:28; Mark 14:24; Luke 22:20; 1 Cor. 11:25; Heb. 12:24; 13:20.

18 "Sons of God" is a rank of angels (who have no gender) and does not exclude women in any way.

covenant do the same, living self-sacrificially and bringing healing and creativity wherever they go. It is a return to the mission given to us by God at the beginning of creation.

Does this sound impossible? It is certainly very hard, and no one keeps it perfectly. But what is impossible for humans by themselves is possible with God (Matt. 19:26). And it is also critical to remember this: Whenever we fail (and we do and we will, over and over), we confess our sins and return to faithfulness to God, and He will clean the sin out from us and return us to righteousness (1 John 1:9).

In ancient pagan societies, forgiveness from the gods was simply not an option. What you got in return for betraying them was revenge or the demand for appeasement. God alone offers forgiveness. If we repent—returning to Him once more—He will forgive, restore, and heal us. Forgiveness is always available, but it is not automatic.

The commandment to "be perfect, just as your Father in heaven is perfect" (Matt. 5:48) also includes instructions on how to become so: love your enemies, be merciful, be honest, and so forth. And it also includes the possibility of repentance. Further, the Holy Spirit—God Himself—is given to us as a gift to enable us to do all these things.

I said above that repentance means to live the angelic life. This description is not a mere metaphor, as we have seen—God's promise to Abraham was that his heirs would be like the angels. In the opening section of Matthew 5, the chapter that concludes with the "be perfect" command, we receive what are called the Beatitudes (Matt. 5:1–12). Each of these lines pronounces a blessing on one of several ways of being faithful: Blessed are the poor in spirit, blessed are those who mourn, blessed are the meek and merciful, and so forth.

Hidden under that English translation *blessed* is the Greek word *makarios*. This is not the usual word, *evlogitos*, which literally means "blessed" (as in having a blessing pronounced on one). *Makarios* is a word from the ancient world that instead referred to the blissful life of the gods in their heavenly realm. It is also used in the Scripture to refer to the joy, the glory, the happiness, the unity, and the love that the faithful angels share with God. Thus, the part of the Lord's prayer that prays that His will should be done "on earth as it is in heaven" is precisely a prayer that He would extend this same blissful happiness to those on earth.

Therefore, turning away from acting like demons and toward acting like angels, away from a hellish life and toward the heavenly one, is the project of being a Christian in this life. It is what the gospel includes as the expectation from those who will be part of the covenant of the coming King.

CHAPTER 6

Responding to the Gospel

*From that time Jesus began to preach and to
say, "Repent, for the kingdom of heaven is at
hand." (Matthew 4:17)*

At the beginning of this book, I said that the gospel was not the answer to the question, "What must I do to be saved?" Rather, the gospel is the proclamation of Christ's victory over His enemies, entailing three points—who He is, what He accomplished, and what He expects of us. We could also describe the gospel as a warning—the Kingdom of God is at hand, so you had better repent.

But if someone believes the gospel and is ready to respond to it, what does he do? And what happens when he responds? What is he being saved from? What does it mean when someone becomes part of the Kingdom of God? These questions are what this final chapter will address. First I will address what those who repent are being saved *from*.

Saved from What?

In order to understand the answers to these questions, we have to return to where we began: A spiritual war is in progress. Some of God's heavenly hosts rebelled against Him and became what we call demons or fallen angels. Those who remained obedient to Him are fighting back against those who rebelled. And God Himself has entered into the fight and cast out those who rebelled.

What does that have to do with us? We have already seen that we live our lives participating in either the demonic army or the angelic one. Someone who believes in the gospel wants to join the angelic army. But what happens to someone who is on the side of the demons?

In the end, when the Day of the Lord comes and Christ is again openly manifest, He will reestablish justice. That means that everything will be set right. All the works of the demons will be undone, and their rebellion places them outside the covenant with God. They will not be in the Kingdom.

You might ask: Why don't they get another chance? It is hard for us to understand, since we cannot really know what it means to be a rebellious demon. But we do know from Scripture and from subsequent Christian tradition that they do not even *want* another chance. Their rebellion is so crystallized that the goodness and love of God is something they simply do not desire. And they are not even capable of changing their minds, because changing one's mind is possible only for those who are able to repent.

I noted before that God gave mortality to humans to enable them to repent. He did not give that to demons. They are immortal in their rebellion. Why does this matter for us?

It matters because, if we choose to participate in the works of demons, we not only become like them, but we will also suffer their fate. The opportunity that God gives us to repent is within the bounds of this current, mortal life. Once we no longer have mortal bodies—after physical

death and even more so after the universal resurrection—*we will not be capable of repentance.*
We will be crystallized in either rebellion or
obedience.

And that is why saints such as Isaac the Syrian said, "This life is given to us for repentance.
Do not waste it on vain pursuits." This life is our
chance.

So this is what being "saved" means. Those
who believe the gospel and repent are being
saved from living for all eternity outside the
Kingdom of God. What that is like is difficult
to say, but with all the images given in Scripture, it is horrifying even to imagine. I think the
best term, though, is probably *insanity.* If the
Kingdom of God is everything made right and
brought into order, then those outside it are in
the opposite state.

What Happens When Someone Is Saved?

We just looked at what happens when someone
joins the losing side in this great spiritual war.
But what happens when someone joins the vic-
tors and remains faithful?

In order to understand that, we have to know

what the angelic life is actually like. People often have an image of angels that is very narrow and even sometimes kind of "cute." First, forget about fat babies with wings. And forget about sentimental glowing blonde women on greeting cards. Angels in the Scripture invoke awe, fear, exultation, and glorification of God in song. And that's just the lower-rank ones who deal directly with mankind.

The higher-ranked angels who guard God's throne—the cherubim and seraphim—are bizarre and utterly frightening to behold. Ancient visions of these beings describe them as sphinxes, as gryphons, as serpents, as strange multi-winged, multi-eyed creatures who surround the very throne of the Most High.

Some of these angels are tasked by God with directly opposing and resisting the demonic hosts. It is written, for instance, that St. Michael the great archangel cast out the draconic demon, the Satan, from the presence of God (Rev. 12:7–9).

But there are also angelic beings who are given the care of the sun, moon, and stars, of the winds and the seas, of all the aspects of creation. Some are assigned to guard and guide nations. And some are assigned to churches, to cities, to monasteries, and even to individual persons. They are the caretakers and stewards of this vast cosmos, including us. Angels do not have material bodies as we do but are vast cosmic intelligences whose existence is beyond our understanding. Yet they are still created beings and should not be worshiped. They are the glorious hosts of heaven.

These heavenly hosts are depicted in Scripture as God's divine council, as in Psalm 82:1 (RSV): "God has taken his place in the divine council." God is therefore also called "God of gods" and "Lord of lords" in many places. He is the Lord of hosts, the Lord of spirits. And no one among these gods (the heavenly hosts) is like Him or worthy of worship. But they all participate in His works and so become like Him in an endless relationship of love.

It is this divine council into which human beings are invited. These heavenly hosts who assist God, who carry out His will, who participate in His glory and in His life, represent the destiny of mankind, the promise given to Abraham that his seed would be as the stars.

When someone becomes part of the divine council, he does not become an angelic being in terms of turning into some other species. Humans remain by nature human. But they take on the same mode of being the angels have, participating in God's love and glory by means of adoption as sons of God, equal to the angels, as Jesus Himself said (Luke 20:36).

This experience is called *theosis*, a word that may be translated "divinization" or "deification." The word refers to this adoption into God's royal family and priesthood. The faithful participate in His life, His works, in Him, and so they become like Him, growing to the stature of the fullness of Christ (Eph. 4:13). Before the time of Christ, this was possible in part through obedience to God, but with the advent of Christ, the gates to this participation are now truly opened.

And being in Him, the faithful become His Body, which means that they function as His powers and influence and work in this world— just as the angels do. It is the work and power of God, but it is accomplished in and through the faithful. That is why, for instance, the mother of Jesus Christ, the Virgin Mary, is called by the Church "more honorable than the cherubim and more glorious beyond compare than the seraphim." By her participation in God's work of incarnation, she has exceeded the glory even of the guardians who stand at God's throne.

This image should dispel any notion that heaven is "boring" (angels sitting around on clouds playing harps) or some kind of sentimental vacation resort for the ethical as a reward for good behavior. No, in the Kingdom of God the faithful "shall be priests of God and of Christ, and shall reign with Him" (Rev. 20:6). Those saved from demonic rebellion do not merely go to some "good place" but become incorporated into the heavenly hosts of the Most High God.

What Must I Do to Be Saved?

Finally we arrive at the question, "What must I do to be saved?" The answer is not easy, but it is simple: Repent, be baptized, and then remain faithful.

We have examined what it means to repent. It means not only to stop behaving demonically by sinning but to begin behaving angelically by acting righteously. Now that we have seen more clearly what the angelic life entails, I hope that the word *angelic* will bear a great weight of responsibility and glory for you. We must make one thing clear: We *cannot* repent and still remain committed to living in sin, to ignoring the commandments of God, to pursuing our own desires instead of His. That is the demonic rebellion, the spirit that says, "Not Thy will, God, but mine." Repentance and turning toward Christ means making a definite break with that demonic allegiance. It does not mean we will never fall again—we will—but we remain committed to getting up every time we fall.

Once that commitment is made, the repentant person approaches the Church[19] to prepare for baptism[20] by contacting the local parish pastor

---

19 Being an Orthodox Christian, I believe and teach that the Church is precisely the Orthodox Church. If you are interested in how the Orthodox Church compares with other Christian and non-Christian groups, see my book *Orthodoxy and Heterodoxy: Finding the Way to Christ in a Complicated Religious Landscape* (Ancient Faith Publishing, 2017). I also discuss there how Orthodox Christians have traditionally understood the status of the non-Orthodox.

20 I will not veer off here into the several ways that someone can be received into the Church depending on their prior religious experience. Baptism is the normal way for the unbaptized. For those whom a local bishop determines to have been baptized already, he may decree other methods in keeping with the historical and canonical traditions of the Church.

and doing as he instructs. After a period of catechesis (instruction in everything he needs to
know to live as a Christian), he is baptized and
begins to receive all the other holy mysteries
(sacraments) of the Church as appropriate—
especially the Eucharist and regular confession.

Partaking of these holy mysteries, continual
growth in repentance (including ascetical train-
ing under the direction of an experienced pastor),
living the angelic life as much as possible while in
this world—this is what it means to be one of the
faithful. And remaining faithful is critical to our
salvation. We cannot be faithful for a while and
then abandon Christ and still expect our prior
faithfulness to keep us united to Him.

We also cannot be faithful by entering the
Church and expecting it to change its teachings
or by defiantly resisting repentance. It is one
thing to struggle with being obedient—we all do
that—but it is another to make the choice to dis-
obey. Faithfulness means making the free choice,
again and again, to be obedient to the commandments of God, and returning to obedience whenever we fail.

Being faithful does not mean that we earn salvation—how could we ever earn life among the

heavenly hosts? But it is what it takes to remain in the Kingdom of Christ. It is the same as faithfulness in a marriage—it is not made or unmade in a single act or by fulfilling a single requirement. It is lived and nurtured and therefore grows and deepens.

And we do not despair, even though we are sinners, because God has given us this great gift, the gift of repentance, the gift of returning to Him again and again. We love Him, and so we keep His commandments.

Repentance is the greatest thing ever accomplished by any human person, which is why it happens only with God's help. There is no higher call, no greater feat, than to turn back to God. It is an act greater than scaling any mountain, curing any bodily disease, conquering any kingdom, creating any masterpiece.

To repent is to be cured of the worst disease ever to infect mankind—sin. To repent is to conquer what is unconquered in so many—the love of oneself above others, an obsession inspired by the demons. To repent is an act of exorcism.

To repent is to become what God has made us to be, the sons of God—to be ranked among the heavenly hosts. To repent is to become the full work of creativity of the great and most high Creator Himself.

Those who repent become as the stars of the heavens, and so enkindled, sing with them the glory of God forever.

The Gospel

I began this little book by talking about the Greek word *evangelion*. To close, I want to say something about the English word *gospel*, because, while English was certainly not in use when the gospel was first preached, I think we can still learn something useful about the gospel by looking at the word we've been using throughout this book.

The English word *gospel* is from our Old English inheritance, that core deposit of the language that English speakers use the most often and which still defines it as a Germanic language. *Gospel* comes from the older form *god-spel*, a "good spell." Like *evangelion*, *gospel* therefore literally means "good news." But look closely and you see the word *spell* in there, too.

We may think of "magic spells." We may think of feelings of foreboding, like "that spells trouble." *Spell* is not just "news," but rather may be thought of as "a word that contains power." We don't have to think of magic spells or impending doom, but we can realize that the gospel is indeed a word of power.

And the Old English *spel* also denotes a story. So the gospel is a narrative, a story that defines what it means to be Christian by telling us who Christ is, what He did, and what He expects of us. But it is also a word of power that both commands our attention and serves as a warning to the demons who have made themselves the enemies of God.

On Holy Saturday, the day before Pascha (Greek for "Passover") or Easter when the Church celebrates our annual participation in the resurrection of Christ, we sing, "Arise, O God, judge the earth, for to Thee belong all the nations!" The defeat of the rebellion has begun, and God's authority over all the earth is being renewed.

God has arisen, and His enemies are scattering because they are being judged by Him. They are opposed by the angelic hosts, the sons of God, who with Christ's power are driving them out in a cosmic act of exorcism. And we are invited to join them.

And so today we make our beginning, setting out on this greatest quest to receive the greatest gift, to learn how to say "Not my will, but Thine," to learn how to become the sons of God.

> *For our gospel did not come to you in*
> *word only, but also in power, and in*
> *the Holy Spirit and in much assurance.*
> *(1 Thessalonians 1:5)*

Acknowledgments

There are four people to whom I owe special thanks for what went into this book. First and second, my parents, Bill and the late Sandy Damick, formed me in love for Jesus Christ. They taught me, by both word and deed, that Christ and His gospel are what matter most and are indeed all that truly matters. What they gave me was no sales pitch but rather a way of both believing and living that truly showed me that the gospel is the very power of God (Rom. 1:16). My mother finished her life speaking of all the blessings that God had given her, even while she was dying untimely (in our eyes) of brain cancer, becoming a gospel proclamation even in her death. She said that God has given each of us something to do, if only we will listen.

The third person is His Eminence, Archbishop

Michael (Dahulich), who was my dean, professor, and confessor during my studies at St. Tikhon's Seminary. I am grateful for his friendship and guidance but most especially for his teaching me the basic model of the gospel message as three points, which I have adapted somewhat here and given some different emphases.

Fourth is my friend and collaborator the Rev. Dr. Stephen De Young, whose biblical scholarship throws open so many doors for me that I can hardly count them. In addition to his critiques of this manuscript, there is so much in this book that owes either its content or its shape to his work that I could almost claim him as a co-author. I am especially indebted to his work on *The Whole Counsel of God* blog and also to the manuscript that I read of *The Religion of the Apostles*, as well as to our many conversations on the *Lord of Spirits* podcast. Rather than footnoting everywhere, I'll note here that with his permission I relied a great deal in many places on the material that became *The Religion of the Apostles* (Ancient Faith Publishing, 2021), and I recommend that book for a fuller treatment of many of the themes I introduce in this volume.

That said, while I am not plagiarizing anyone,

I make no apologies for not being original. If there is anything one does not want to be original about, it's the gospel. But I do hope that my particular way of communicating it to you will be effective.

I am also grateful to the others who looked at this book's manuscript and provided valuable comments and corrections: the team at Ancient Faith Publishing, who believed with me in this book and gave it the polish needed, as well as Fr. Anthony Cook, Fr. Paul Hodge, Fr. Anthony Perkins, Fr. Alexandros Petrides, Pdn. David Keim, Katherine Psaropoulou Brits, Ben Cabe, Jonathan Jackson, Matthew Namee, and Richard Rohlin.

Finally, I want to say something about (and to) my daughter Evangelia, to whom this book is dedicated. I hope she will read it. I truly dedicate this work to her, which is to say that she is the first for whose sake I write these things. My own parents gave me this greatest gift—Jesus Christ—and if I can give that same gift to my firstborn, who is named for the very gospel, then I may count myself a Christian and a father.

I love all my children and commend this same gift to all of them equally, but Evangelia, by

God's grace, you will always get to go first. See to it, my daughter, that you are also first among the givers of this gift of *evangelion*. It is your inheritance and your birthright. May both your name and your life openly proclaim this greatest of all news to all who know you.

The Very Rev. Archpriest Andrew Stephen Damick is Chief Content Officer of Ancient Faith Ministries, the former pastor (2009–2020) of St. Paul Antiochian Orthodox Church of Emmaus, Pennsylvania, and author of several books from Ancient Faith Publishing: *Orthodoxy and Heterodoxy, An Introduction to God,* and *Bearing God*. He hosts the podcasts *Orthodox Engagement* and *Amon Sûl* and co-hosts *The Lord of Spirits* and *The Areopagus*. He resides in Emmaus with his wife, Kh. Nicole, and their children.

For Further Reading & Listening

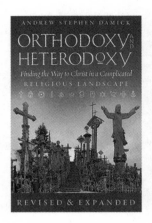

Are you an Ortho-dox Christian who wonders how to explain to your Baptist grand-mother, your Buddhist neighbor, or the Jeho-vah's Witness at your door how your faith differs from theirs? Or are you a member of another faith who is curious what Orthodoxy is all about? Look no further. In *Orthodoxy & Heterodoxy*, Fr. Andrew Stephen Damick covers the gamut of ancient her-esies, modern Christian denominations, fringe groups, and major world religions, highlighting the main points of each faith. This book is an invaluable reference for anyone who wants to understand the faiths of those they come in con-tact with—as well as their own.

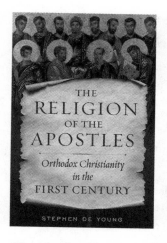

Father Dr. Stephen De Young traces the lineage of Orthodox Christianity back to the faith and witness of the apostles, which was rooted in a first-century Jewish worldview. *The Religion of the Apostles* presents the Orthodox Christian Church of today as a continuation of the religious life of the apostles, which in turn was a continuation of the life of the people of God since the beginning of creation.

With this book, Fr. Stephen De Young is not only leading the charge for Orthodox apologetics in a world of secular biblical scholarship, but he is also doing us all a favor by reviving the cosmic frame of ancient Christians, giving hope to a jaded culture desperately looking for a re-enchanted world in which it can fully participate.

—Jonathan Pageau, The Symbolic World

The Seen and Unseen World in Orthodox Christian Tradition

The modern world doesn't acknowledge but is nevertheless haunted by spirits—angels, demons, and saints.

Orthodox Christian priests Fr. Andrew Stephen Damick and Fr. Stephen De Young host this live call-in show focused on enchantment in creation, the union of the seen and unseen as made by God and experienced by mankind throughout history.

What is spiritual reality like? How do we engage with it well? How do we permeate everyday life with spiritual presence?

The live edition of this show airs on the second and fourth Thursdays of the month at 7 pm ET / 4 pm PT. Tune in at ancientfaith.com.

Other Podcasts Featuring
Fr. Andrew Stephen Damick

Exploring the Tolkien
Legendarium with the
Christian Faith

Historic Christianity
Encounters Other
Religious Traditions

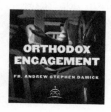

Not to Condemn the
World, But to Save It

Ancient Faith Publishing hopes you have enjoyed and benefited from this book. The proceeds from the sales of our books only partially cover the costs of operating our nonprofit ministry—which includes both the work of **Ancient Faith Publishing** and the work of **Ancient Faith Radio**. Your financial support makes it possible to continue this ministry both in print and online. Donations are tax deductible and can be made at **www.ancientfaith.com**.

To view our other publications,
please visit our website:
store.ancientfaith.com

Bringing you Orthodox Christian music,
readings, prayers, teaching, and podcasts
24 hours a day since 2004 at
www.ancientfaith.com